ADVERSARIES
into ALLIES

ALSO BY BOB BURG

Endless Referrals: Network Your Everyday Contacts into Sales
The Art of Persuasion: Winning Without Intimidation
The Success Formula

BY BOB BURG AND JOHN DAVID MANN

The Go-Giver: A Little Story About a Powerful Business Idea
Go-Givers Sell More
It's Not About You: A Little Story About What Matters
Most in Business

ADVERSARIES
into ALLIES

Win People Over Without Manipulation or Coercion

BOB BURG

Portfolio / Penguin

PORTFOLIO / PENGUIN
Published by the Penguin Group
Penguin Group (USA) LLC
375 Hudson Street
New York, New York 10014

USA | Canada | UK | Ireland | Australia | New Zealand | India | South Africa | China
penguin.com
A Penguin Random House Company

First published by Portfolio / Penguin, a member of Penguin Group (USA) LLC, 2013

ISBN: 978-1-59184-636-9
Printed in the United States of America

1 3 5 7 9 10 8 6 4 2

Set in Minion Pro
Designed by Elyse Strongin

Thank you, Mom and Dad,
for being such an amazing example of what parents
are supposed to be.

And, thank you, Dad,
for being the best mentor a son could ever have.
This book is my way of carrying on your legacy.

CONTENTS

SECTION THREE

Understand the Clash of Belief Systems
Avoiding Those Deadly Misunderstandings 59

SECTION SEVEN

The Character of Ultimate Influencers
Even More Important Than What You Say and What You Do Is Who You Are   221

NOTE ON THE TEXT

The author feels very strongly regarding the utilization of gender equality in his writing. The pronouns his and her, he and she, et cetera, have been used interchangeably and randomly throughout the text.

ADVERSARIES
into ALLIES

INTRODUCTION

> Who is Mighty? Those who can control their own emotions and make
> of an enemy a friend.
>
> —*Talmud,* Pirkei Avos (Wisdom of the Fathers)

You can have practically every positive trait working for you—you can be talented, of high character, ambitious, kind, charitable, hardworking, thrifty, and energetic. You can have a knack for numbers and a head for business, you can be even-tempered, creative, et cetera.

However . . .

Unless you are able to influence the way others think and act, your chances for success in any aspect of your life are limited.

No, this has nothing to do with manipulating others. It does mean that with both benevolent intent and ability you can consistently obtain both personal and business satisfaction while making others' lives significantly better.

I call this Ultimate Influence: the ability to get the results you want from others while making them feel *genuinely* good about themselves, about the process, and about you.

We're about to take a journey that will include five immediately actionable principles to make your life more fun, less stressful, and a *lot* more profitable! And as you do this, you'll become better liked and more respected, and you'll know that you've made a terrific, positive difference in your world.

As the opening quote describes, only when you can subdue your own emotions are you in a position of true strength, of true influence. Indeed, you are then so powerful you can transform a potentially negative situation into a win for all involved.

While there is certainly more to Ultimate Influence than simply controlling your emotions, it begins there.

The dictionary defines adversary as "a person, group, or force that opposes or attacks; opponent; enemy; foe." But when I use the term adversaries in the title of this book, I am not talking about actual enemies. And, you might not like to think of people who are not immediately on your side as adversaries. That's fair.

I don't take the word adversary in the literal sense, but use the term to refer to those who—regardless of their intentions—stand in the way of our personal satisfaction. They are a part of our learning process—not negative figures, but necessary ones. Just as the great Japanese home-run hitter Sadaharu Oh viewed opposing pitchers as his "partners in hitting home runs," I see adversaries as our partners in growth and success—and as people we can turn into allies for mutual gain.

These partners take different forms, playing a part in many of life's different situations. They range from family members to well-intentioned friends, and can include coworkers, employees, supervisors, employers, team members, committee members, salespeople, prospects, customers, clients, bureaucrats, customer service representatives, and many, many others.

People can be difficult, or *adversarial*. Sometimes you need to find a win/win solution to dealing with a person you already know is difficult. Other times it's important to make sure that a potentially difficult person doesn't become an adversary in the first place. This book will help you do both.

After seeing the title, some early readers asked if this is a book about negotiation. Only in the sense that we negotiate our way through everything in life in one way or another. So while it is not about the topic of negotiation or about specific negotiation skills and tactics, you'll find it to be beneficial in all of your dealings with others, including direct negotiations.

Because of my background in sales and teaching selling skills, another excellent question I've received is, "Is this a book on selling?" While some of the examples in these pages will deal directly with the selling process, it's not a book on selling per se. Again, only in the sense that if we understand that selling is about moving others to accept our ideas—whether we're deciding which movie to see with a friend, selling our product to a new prospect, or trying to get better service from a difficult rep—we are selling on a constant basis.

So, what *is* this book really about?

Adversaries into Allies is about mastering one specific area of success. It's one that has proven itself again and again to be the determining factor between the average or reasonably successful person and the one who is able to accomplish great and significant levels of achievement. And that is *people skills*.

Indeed, there are certainly those who've attained great financial success *despite* their lack of people skills. But they've achieved what they have in spite of this, *not* because of it. For many of these people, their personal relationships were and are a mess. Still, because of some other powerful qualities, they have achieved—at least financially—some huge success. Even though such examples are rare, they do happen.

Most of us, on the other hand, need very powerful people skills to succeed not only in business but in all areas of life.

I believe that success in life is based on 10 percent technical skills and 90 percent people skills.

Of course, technical skills are *hugely* important. Talent counts; ability counts; competence counts. However, they are simply the baseline—they get you into the game. Some of the most talented people in the world accomplish very average results because they have not mastered the people skills and influence skills that elicit the necessary action, buy in, or commitment from others.

How much more effective do you feel you would be with people—whether they're friends or loved ones, colleagues or customers—if you mastered Ultimate Influence?

If you already excel in this area, you're going to enjoy the principles we look at in *Adversaries into Allies* because they will make you even more effective than you already are. If, on the other hand, you feel as though your influence and persuasion skills are currently *not* among your strengths, you are going to *really* enjoy what you're about to read.

The information in this book will open up a whole new world for you in terms of both your personal and professional effectiveness. You'll also quickly see that these concepts are pretty simple to grasp.

As you know, simple doesn't always mean easy. However, one of the key aspects in terms of learning my Ultimate Influence Principles is that they are easy to put into practice. You will find them so intuitive that applying them will be natural, easy, and very, very fun.

So let's get started!

SECTION ONE

The Five Principles of Ultimate Influence

Understand These and You'll Understand the Basics of All Human Action and Interaction

Highly respected leadership authority Dr. John C. Maxwell says, "Influence is everything." That's a pretty bold statement. Yet I believe it is true.

Before I can explain why, however, I first need to define *influence*.

At the most basic level, influence is the ability to move a person or persons to a desired action, usually within the context of a specific goal. While that's a pretty good definition, it doesn't tell the full story. The key to the kind of influence I'm talking about—what I call Ultimate Influence—encompasses not only the ability to move someone to action but the *manner in which you move them*. In other words, not just *what* you do but *how* you do it.

Truly successful individuals create both immediate and long-lasting influence attracting others to them. After all, there's a reason we say that someone with influence has a lot of "pull." Great influencers attract people, both to themselves and to their ideas.

When you think about it, there are only two ways to move a person to change their thoughts or take the action you wish for them to take: by force or persuasion.

Have you ever witnessed an intimidating boss? Did people do their best work for him or her, giving every project 100 percent? Probably not. Chances are they did the bare minimum, at best performing only well enough to keep their job.

When people are treated less than respectfully, or simply forced to do something, they will comply, but begrudgingly. At best, they will do exactly what they're told to do and not one bit more. At worst, they'll find a way to sabotage the process completely—consciously or unconsciously.

Indeed, force can work to a point, but as soon as the person in charge loses his *positional authority*, his ability to force others to action is gone. In other words, force is rarely, if ever, sustainable.

Persuasion, on the other hand, is much more effective because, by definition, it requires that the person acts on their own volition. When you persuade someone, you don't force them to comply with your wishes, but rather you help them see why their desired outcome and your desired outcome are the same. Not only is the immediate result of higher quality but future good results are almost assured.

It's All About Them

Let's go back to the idea of creating allies. What is an ally? An ally is a partner; someone who shares your goals or has similar ones. Allies are not subordinate; they are equals who *choose* to align themselves with you because they know that doing so will benefit them in at least some way. This holds true whether we are talking about a team of thousands, a small group, or even just one person.

Great leaders—Ultimate Influencers—embrace what I believe was one of Dale Carnegie's most profoundly wise statements in his classic book *How to Win Friends and Influence People*: "Ultimately, people do things for their reasons, not our reasons."

In becoming an Ultimate Influencer, it is so important that you understand, embrace, and keep this law of human nature at the top of your mind.

Indeed, all actions we as human beings take are based on self-interest.

"What?" you may ask. "What about charity and other forms of altruism? Are you trying to say that is based on self-interest, as well?"

Actually, yes! Everyone's actions are ultimately based on self-interest. Even when giving charity (even when you donate a kidney!), you do this because it aligns with your personal value system; you believe it is the right thing to do, and it makes you feel good about yourself.

It's Human Nature . . . and It's Okay

I understand that this concept challenges some long-assumed premises. And this by no means is meant to imply that every choice one makes is the easiest, most comfortable, or most convenient—only that one does it for *their* own reasons, either consciously or unconsciously, based on their own personal value system.

I stress this point regarding self-interest because understanding it is perhaps the key to mastering Ultimate Influence; understanding that the other person will do what they are going to do for *their* reasons, not yours.

If your request is not mandatory (and, as we've seen, compliance is a weak and generally ineffective form of influence), you must give the other individual a personal benefit for taking action. Present your request with that in mind.

Are you planning to ask your boss for a raise? Telling her you are behind on your house payment and that you really *need* the money will probably not motivate her to agree. You're much better served explaining that, based on past performance, you could help her come in significantly under budget on the next project. That, of course, would make her look great to her superiors when she is seeking *her* raise.

Do you want your prospect to buy from you? He isn't going to do it because you need to make your quota. The chances of a sale taking place are considerably greater if you can tie his wants and needs with the benefits that your product or service provides.

And do you want the unhelpful person at the customer service desk to go out of her way for you when it's not something required in her job description? Then you'd better somehow ensure that she sees it as being to her advantage to overcome their inertia and usual disinterest.

Important point: everyone's motivation is not necessarily money. The vast majority of time it is not. Feeling good about oneself is often the most powerful motivator of all! Difficult people, in particular, tend to have a poor self-image. So take a genuine, personal interest in them. Show more respect than they might typically receive. Find out what will press their emotional hot button and cause them to take the action you want them to take. Ask yourself, *What's in it for them*?

If you nail that answer, chances are that they—or anyone else— will bend over backward to make you happy.

That's Ultimate Influence!

The Law of Influence

In *The Go-Giver*, my coauthor, John David Mann, and I introduced "The Law of Influence," which states: "Your influence is determined by how abundantly you place other people's interests first."

While that perhaps sounds counterproductive at best, and downright *Pollyanna-ish* at worst, it's really how most great leaders, top influencers, and highly profitable salespeople conduct their lives and run their businesses.

Please do not misinterpret this. When we say, "place other people's interests first," we're not suggesting you should be anyone's doormat, a martyr, or in any way self-sacrificial. Not at all. People who let other people take advantage of them are acting out of weakness, not out of strength, and can never be truly influential.

However, consciously shifting your focus away from yourself is about the very best way you can ever influence another.

The basic premise of everything I teach in terms of selling is that:

> All things being equal, people will do business with, and refer business to, those people they know, like, and trust.

Influence, both in and out of business, is a form of selling. You are selling your thoughts, opinions, needs, desires, philosophies, and more. Therefore, remember that:

> All things being equal, people will do business with, refer business to, *and allow themselves to be influenced by* those people they know, like, and trust.

And the fastest, most powerful, and most effective way to elicit like and trust toward you from others is via that all-important shift from an "I or me" focus to an "other" focus.

Master this shift in focus and you will have separated yourself from the majority of people on this planet who try to influence others while focusing only on themselves.

Most people don't commit to things; they commit to people. And they typically commit to people who they believe care about *them*.

And that is where I am in full agreement with Dr. Maxwell's statement. In terms of accomplishing a goal—and knowing that most goals are accomplished only with the help, support, and commitment of others—influence is indeed everything.

This is not to say that influence—doing it and having it—is always a positive thing. For it to be positive it must come from a place of benevolent (at best) or benign (at worst) intent, and it must also help the person who is being influenced. Otherwise, we're probably talking about manipulation.

That's why the *way* one influences is so very important. Persuasion or manipulation, commitment or compliance, power or force. Each one is an either/or. It's a choice; it's a mindset. It's also a skill set.

Once you learn how to influence in a way that you consistently and almost predictably obtain the results you want while making others feel good about themselves, you'll discover a far more effective and lasting way than any force, compliance, or manipulation could ever possibly accomplish.

THE FIVE PRINCIPLES

Ultimate Influence is based on five key principles that occur on an ongoing basis.

In any interpersonal transaction where you desire to move a person to a different thought or action than they otherwise would take without your influence, you'll need to do one or more of the following (and often all five).

1. Control your own emotions
2. Understand the clash of belief systems
3. Acknowledge their ego
4. Set the proper frame
5. Communicate with tact and empathy

Control Your Own Emotions

Only when we are in control of our own emotions are we able to act out of thought, out of consciousness, and help create a situation in which everyone involved can come away as winners.

Human beings are emotional creatures. Most of us like to think of ourselves as logical—and to a certain degree we are—but, by and large, we act out of emotion.

We make major decisions based on emotion and then back up those emotional decisions with logic.

How do we do that? We rationalize. If you break up the word rationalize you get "rational lies." Yes, we make our decisions based mostly upon our emotions and then back up these decisions with those rational lies we tell ourselves.

Rational lie: "Even though I can't afford it, I really need that luxury car that costs me an extra few hundred dollars per month, is more expensive to insure, and is worse on gas. Why? Because, my prospects need to see me as successful. In fact, just one additional sale per month will pay for it."

The truth: "I want everyone to think I'm financially successful and I feel better about myself when driving a cool car."

Rational lie: "It's important for me to know what's happening in the personal lives of my coworkers and to make sure I keep others in the loop, as well. After all, someone's personal life can affect both the working environment and the bottom line."

The truth: "I like to partake in gossip both as a listener and a speaker."

These seem like simple examples, but if someone you know has used either of the above rationalizations, chances are they would not accept my analysis. When a person believes something strongly and you suggest they are wrong, how likely is it that—based on *logic* alone—they will agree with you? Not very likely. They will find reasons not to. And they may not even realize they are doing this.

As Daniel Goleman discussed in his classic *Emotional Intelligence*, "The emotional mind . . . takes its beliefs to be absolutely true, and so discounts any evidence to the contrary. That is why it is so hard to reason with someone who is emotionally upset: no matter the sound-

THE FIVE PRINCIPLES | 13 |

ness of your argument from a logical point of view, it carries no weight if it is out of keeping with the emotional conviction of the moment."

Goleman adds, and I believe this is one of the most important things to understand: "Feelings are self-justifying, with a set of perceptions and 'proofs' all their own."

And when ruled by self-justification we are nowhere near as effective as we could be.

Lest you think I'm asking you to turn yourself into an unemotional and non-feeling machine, please know that is not the case. Embrace your emotions. However, as leadership authority Dondi Scumaci says:

> "Emotions are important for the journey . . . but I don't let them drive the car!"

Ahhh. *That* is the key. The point is not to turn ourselves into a bunch of robots. Emotion is one of the vital ingredients to a wonderful life, but it's important that you are at the steering wheel.

Be sure that your emotions don't drive *you*; you drive *them*. You are at the steering wheel, and they are in the passenger's seat, safety belt in place.

When you can both master your emotions and *help* others to work effectively within theirs, your level of influence will be sky high.

In section two we will explore this first principle of Ultimate Influence. You'll learn how to respond instead of react, smoothly handle verbal attacks, make calmness your default setting, detach from and defuse your anger, make silence your best friend, and more.

Understand the Clash of Belief Systems

Have you ever crossed signals with a friend and learned, only after it was too late, that you both unquestioningly assigned very *different meanings* to the exact same word; hence the confusion? "Oh, I thought you wanted to meet at the actual beach—next to the ocean—not the new restaurant called The Beach!"

Have you ever lost a sale because while you were certain that your prospect was bothered by a certain issue (let's say the price), she wasn't? You discovered only after it was too late that her actual concern was something totally different.

And have you ever had an anger-filled disagreement with someone only to later learn that it was based totally and completely on a misunderstanding?

If you're like most people, your answer is a definite "Yes!" That's why the second principle of Ultimate Influence is determining how to get out of your own head and into the mind of the person you're trying to influence.

Later, we'll discover why this situation is so prevalent and learn a method you can use to overcome it, making your level of communication far more effective and your success more assured.

Each one of us sees the world in a unique way based on a combination of upbringing, environment, schooling, popular media, and the people with whom we associate. And such is the case with the person in front of you.

Your potential adversary doesn't realize that he sees the world based on his belief system, but believes that everyone else sees the world about the same way he does. He is totally unaware of this.

So he interprets our words and actions in light of his belief system, not ours. And we do the exact same thing.

Even when we know this, we typically operate without being conscious of it.

Think about it: your life is also run by a belief system based on the same factors as the person's you are attempting to effectively influence. And the same rules that apply to their deep-set belief system, apply to *yours* as well.

Do you see where a clash might occur?

Until you understand this and are able to operate based on this awareness, you could easily find yourself stuck in a quagmire of non-understanding, which, more often than not, leads to a misunderstanding.

In section three you'll learn that you don't necessarily have to understand their belief system; you can start simply by understanding that their belief system is very likely different from yours. Then you will be more able to work successfully within that context. You'll discover ways to ensure you're both on the same page, how to avoid unhelpful assumptions, how not to take things personally, and get additional insights into this very important concept.

Acknowledge Their Ego

Some dignitaries were attending a formal and very fancy black-tie affair at a major Washington, D.C., hotel. One of the guests, a United States senator, noticed that at his table setting there was only a single pat of butter next to his roll.

Dismissively, and with a wag of his index finger, he summoned the waiter. "Young man, bring me another pat of butter."

A bit taken aback but having to feign politeness, the waiter replied, "I'm sorry, sir, it's only one pat of butter per setting."

Annoyed, the self-important politician said, "I want another one anyway; bring me another pat of butter right now."

"I'm sorry," countered the waiter. "We're a bit short tonight; it's just one pat of butter per setting."

Now totally put off and offended, the VIP demanded, "Young man, do you know who I am? I happen to be the senior senator from the state of New Jersey."

"And do you know who I am?" the waiter replied. "I'm the guy who controls the butter."

I doubt this ever actually happened, but I love this story because it perfectly illustrates the ego at work. Most people would look at this senator and think he has a large ego because of his sense of entitlement. But as we see, the waiter has an ego, too.

We usually think of ego as a bad thing—a problem that self-involved, narcissistic people suffer from. But the ego is nothing more than one's sense of self. Everyone has that, and if you bruise it by failing to acknowledge another person's sense of self, you'll have a hard time winning that person over.

If the senator really wanted that extra pat of butter, as minor a request as it seemed to him, he would have done better to focus on the waiter's ego, which *must* be honored throughout the process. After all, it will come into play whether or not you think it should.

I wholeheartedly believe:

> About 95 percent of the time, being able to move a person to
> your side of an issue comes down to how you make him (or
> help him) feel about himself.

The ego is the ultimate driving force in everything people do. And as with their belief system, they are more than likely totally and completely unaware that this operating system is in play even as they go about their lives and deal with others.

This is not to say the ego is only a negative aspect of the human entity. When controlled, the ego can be put to great use, both for individual accomplishment and societal good.

Still, we need to understand this when dealing with others: their ego is highly sensitive, and if you want someone to agree with your wishes, you must handle it with extreme caution and care.

Of course, you, too, are driven by *your* ego. So you must also be aware of yours if you want to work successfully with theirs.

Yes, awareness of the ego is important. But it's *your* awareness that is key. More than likely, the other person is not aware. The onus is on you.

In section four you will learn more about how to control your ego and acknowledge and work with the conscious and unconscious effects of other people's egos.

Set the Proper Frame

Imagine you are in a store and you watch a disgruntled customer bark, "This is unacceptable! I demand to see the manager right now!"

Two minutes later the manager appears. He is calm and steadied, but obviously prepared for a battle and ready to quote "company policy" as soon as he possibly can.

Now picture how that scene might play out with some small but important changes. This time the customer quickly reins in his frustration and says to the cashier, "I'm sorry to have to put you in this position. It might be better if I speak to the manager. What's his or her name?"

Two minutes later, the manager appears. He is calm and feeling neutral, having been told that the customer needing to speak with him is very nice. Still, policy is policy and he's prepared to quote it if necessary.

With a warm smile and an outstretched hand, the customer says, "Hi, Mr. Jones, I'm Pat Thomas. Thank you so much for coming out to speak with me. I know you're very busy."

The manager, much less concerned with company policy, now wonders how he can best serve the very type of customer that every business wants to have.

What is a frame? Basically, it's the premise, the context from which everything else in your interpersonal transactions takes place.

We just witnessed two of them. And both types occur countless times per day throughout the world. However, as you well know, scene one is much, *much* more common than scene two. The main difference between the two lies in how the frame was set. In the first one, a frame of conflict was set by both parties, so each expected the other to be combative and acted accordingly. In the second one, the customer set a frame of helpfulness, which influenced the manager to be helpful as well. Who do you think would meet with better results?

During every potential interpersonal conflict, a frame *will* be set. The only question is, who will set the frame? If you allow the other person to, you are taking the chance that she understands this concept (she probably doesn't) and that she will set a frame that serves you (she won't). If you set the frame, you are in control. Do this correctly and you have—in essence—determined the entire direction of the transaction.

We'll see plenty of examples of this throughout the book. Keep noticing the "frame games" being played. In section five we'll dive deeper into this topic and learn the real reason setting positive expectations works, why you *should* sometimes let them see you sweat, and other strategies for taking this important step toward becoming an Ultimate Influencer.

Communicate with Tact and Empathy

My Dad, Mike Burg, says, "Tact is the language of strength." Communicating tactfully displays a genuine regard for the other person, which will open the door to making him your ally. It's also somewhat of a linchpin in that—without it—your other skills will be rendered much less effective. The ability to use tact in every situation is key to becoming an Ultimate Influencer.

Tact is the ability to say something in a way that makes the other person feel less threatened or defensive and more open to you and your ideas. This is powerful. Rather than bruising their ego and eliciting the usual resentful feelings and resistance most people can display in this situation, tact opens them up to very positively accepting your suggestion, and acting upon it!

Complaining loudly that your steak is underdone and curtly demanding it to be redone will be far less effective at getting the waitstaff on your side than gently calling over the waiter and with a genuine smile and appreciative tone saying: "The meal is delicious and I love the presentation of it. The meat is just a bit undercooked. Could you let the chef know how much I'm enjoying it, and if she could cook it just a tiny bit more that would terrific?"

Saying the right thing *and* saying it correctly brings forth results that seem like magic. The good news is that communicating with tact is a skill you will easily learn through this book. At first you may have to work at consciously utilizing it, but stick with it and it will soon become a natural part of your being. You'll be amazed at how far a little bit of tact goes in influencing others.

Empathy is related to tact but can be defined as the ability to identify with another's feelings.

Is empathy simply putting yourself in the other person's shoes? Not exactly. Even if we have shared another person's experience, our aforementioned individual belief systems, personalities, convictions, and the variety of our backgrounds makes each person's reaction, even to common experiences, different.

Fortunately, in order to communicate empathy, you don't necessarily have to understand exactly *how* they feel. All you need is to communicate that you understand they're feeling *something*; something that is uncomfortable for them, and that you are there to help them work through it.

Like tact, feeling and communicating empathy for another person is a skill that you can develop. It is vitally important to becoming an Ultimate Influencer, and we'll talk about the two traits together because they tend to work hand in hand. You will naturally display tact when you are truly empathetic to another's situation. And speaking tactfully will communicate your empathy to that person.

In section six we will dive into the nuts and bolts of becoming a more tactful and empathetic communicator—the final and crucial principle in your Ultimate Influence tool kit. You'll learn how to open a conversation to get what you need, give the other person an out, say no without damaging a relationship, handle an interrupter with aplomb, and many more aspects of this skill.

Every principle, strategy, and methodology within this book will assist you in mastering the above five principles. You'll see that when you begin to control your emotions, consider others' points of view and ego, create a positive atmosphere, and communicate tactfully and with empathy, you will get what you want in your personal interactions and relationships. Additionally, you will be able to make the other person feel genuinely good as well, so you both come away winners.

Each of the next five sections of the book is dedicated to taking a closer look at the five principles of Ultimate Influence and offering strategies to avoid common pitfalls as well as provide lots of real-world examples. You'll often sense that chapters, stories, and examples within one principle seem to relate to another principle (and you'd be correct). The keys to solving many—if not most—of the situations you'll face require using more than one of the five principles. Throughout the book I've simply included the scenarios I felt were most relevant to that principle.

After exploring the five principles in detail, we'll take a look at that which ultimately creates Ultimate Influence—the character of the influencer. After all, when it comes right down to it, your influence is determined even more by who you *are*, than by what you say and do.

IT'S (MUCH) MORE
THAN JUST ABOUT BEING NICE

Do nice people really finish last? No, not necessarily.

Do nice people then finish first? No, not necessarily.

In becoming influential, being nice is certainly helpful. After all, who wouldn't rather befriend, interact, and do business with nice people than nasty ones? However, being nice is not enough to be successful in most areas of life, including our dealings with others.

Of course, people with good interpersonal skills typically *are* nice and genuinely kind (the terms nice and kind are not necessarily the same; one could act nice when it suited them but not be very kind at heart). But, again, there's a lot more to influence than simply being nice. We all know people who we would describe as nice but not as particularly influential or successful.

Having influence and obtaining success of any kind is a matter of doing the correct things in the correct way. Nice is indeed helpful. But it's not enough.

We often hear people complain that they are so nice that they get taken advantage of. Please remove that possibility from your mind. There is absolutely no natural correlation between being nice and being taken advantage of.

If you are one of these nice people who find themselves being co-erced, manipulated, and otherwise taken advantage of, the following might be one of the most important statements you will ever read.

> People take advantage of you not because you are nice, but because you *allow yourself to be taken advantage of.*

As you go through this book, you'll learn how to get what you want. I will show you how you can—and you must!—be both nice and kind while doing it. And you will *not* be taken advantage of.

The key is that everyone comes away a winner and—just as important—*feeling* like a winner. Keep in mind though, when you do this correctly, you will receive what you want; mainly, the willing and enthusiastic cooperation of others.

Ultimate Influence is about getting what you want while making others feel good about themselves. In doing so, you persuade them to act in your favor.

PERSUASION
VERSUS MANIPULATION

But wait just a minute, Burg! When you say we persuade others to act, that sounds an awful lot like manipulation.

I'm often asked to explain the difference between *persuasion* and *manipulation*. Actually, it tends to take more the form of a challenge, as in, "Bob, aren't persuasion and manipulation the same thing?"

And it's a good, legitimate question. Persuasion and manipulation are certainly cousins, and to deny that is to deny reality. In both cases, you are attempting to move an individual or group of individuals to think or do something they would presumably not think or do without your influence.

Persuasion, like the verb form of influence, is really nothing more than the ability to move a person to adjust their thoughts and/or actions. We influence through persuasion or manipulation—the one being good and the other being evil. When we influence with benevolent or even benign intent, that's fine. But what about when it is not? What if a person's goal is to cause another human being harm, or (more commonly) if they simply don't care whether harm occurs so long as they get their own way?

Both persuasion and manipulation are based on certain principles of human action and interaction. Good persuaders—and good manipulators—understand those principles and know how to effectively utilize them. That's why . . .

> There is perhaps nothing more dangerous than a bad person with good people skills.

Yes, the principles and methods are similar, at times even the same. In reality, however, the results are as different as night and day.

The Big Difference Is in the Intent

In his 1986 book, *The Art of Talking So That People Will Listen,* Dr. Paul W. Swets provided an outstanding explanation regarding both intent and outcome. He wrote:

> Manipulation aims at control, not cooperation. It results in a win/lose situation. It does not consider the good of the other party. Persuasion is just the opposite. In contrast to the manipulator, the persuader seeks to enhance the self-esteem of the other party. The result is that people respond better because they are treated as responsible, self-directing individuals.

Persuasion aims to serve; manipulation, to hurt. Or even if not necessarily intending to hurt, certainly not caring *if* it does. The manipulator is simply so focused on their own self-interest that they do *only* what they feel is for their own benefit. If someone must suffer as a result, so be it.

What manipulators don't realize is that not only is this not good life practice, it's not good *business.*

A manipulator can have employees but never a team.

She can have customers but rarely ones who will be long lasting and a source of referrals. And once the manipulator is *discovered*, her customer base tends to crumble like a stale cookie.

He can have friends and family but rarely are these relationships fulfilling and happy. Instead, they tend to be guarded in suspicion and filled with resentment.

Yes, both persuaders and manipulators know the how and why of human motivation. And both utilize their knowledge to cause the action they desire a person to take.

However, the crucial difference between the two is that while manipulators use that knowledge to *their* advantage only, the persuader uses it to the *other* person's advantage as well.

The Telltale Signs of Manipulation

How do you know when someone is attempting to manipulate *you*? And, how can you check yourself to make sure you are not unintentionally doing the same to someone else?

Although manipulation and persusasion are based on similar principles, there is something that a manipulator will often do that a persuader will *never* do, and it's important you are aware of it. After all, part of being a great influencer is knowing how *not* to fall victim to that which you would also never intentionally do to others.

> A manipulator will play on your negative emotions in order to elicit your compliance.

In other words, if you fail to comply with his request, a manipulator will try to make you feel bad, selfish, naive, foolish, guilty, or whatever emotion will cause you to capitulate to their desire. He'll try to push your buttons so that you'll do anything to get relief from those negative feelings—including capitulating to his desires despite your best judgment.

So how can you tell when someone is trying to manipulate you? It's actually very easy to recognize.

1. You feel any of the negative emotions mentioned above.
2. You are being asked to do something that you simply would not do of your own choosing or free will.

The good news is you do have free will and you absolutely can refuse.

In every interaction, even with those you love and trust, be conscious of what is taking place. If you feel any type of negative emotions as you're about to "do the thing," ask yourself why. You'll know the answer.

And as far as refusing? In section six, on tact and empathy, we'll discuss how to say no graciously. You'll learn how to do this effectively while being kind, and *without* the need for excuses. If you have a pattern of saying yes when you really want to say no, this will be a game changer for you.

By the way, manipulation comes in varying degrees and isn't always of malicious intent. Actually, in rare but important instances it's not even a negative thing. Hey, if it's a matter of needing to manipulate someone in order to save their life or set up an intervention for a drug-addicted friend or relative, by all means, do whatever you reasonably need to do. No thinking person would most likely say otherwise.

But even in cases where manipulation could lead to good results and could be forgivable, it's still manipulation and it's never the ideal course of action.

For instance, the person who wants you to serve on a committee won't take no for an answer. She's far from evil, but she is trying to guilt-trip you. She really believes in the importance of this committee and that you are the right person to serve on it. As far as she is concerned, it's simply the right thing for you to do, even if you don't want to.

She may not even realize she is being manipulative. She just wants you to do it and is handling the situation the best way she knows how.

Often, people resort to manipulation because they truly don't know how to effectively persuade.

Family and friends are sometimes the most guilty of manipulation. They love you and want only what they believe is best for you. They don't feel you should leave your secure job in order to strike out on your own. And they are reminding you of a past failure or two just to make sure their point hits home.

Here again, their tactics are what's negative, not their intent.

But it's still manipulation. Of course, I'm not saying whether or not you should serve on a committee. And I'm not saying you shouldn't listen to your friends or family members. I'm only suggesting that if you do, it should be because you consciously choose to and it is congruent with your values and desires; not because you were manipulated into doing it.

Persuader, Watch Thyself!

When using our influence, we must always be aware of our own motives and the difference between positive persuasion and negative manipulation.

We're only human, and as such we can rationalize even the most egregious manipulation as "harmless" or "for their own good." When we want something badly enough, it's easy to rationalize. And sometimes it's difficult to notice those "rational lies" we might tell ourselves.

An Ultimate Influencer stays constantly aware of this. Ask yourself, *Am I doing something that will in any way hurt that person or be contrary to their best interests?* (Careful—don't *"rational lies"* that one, as well.)

When trying to sell a good or service, a common rationalization is that you are doing it for *their* benefit. This is tricky because, well, who are we to decide that?

However, that isn't the whole story. Maybe you are sure your product or service would benefit them. In that case it actually *is* your responsibility to *persuade* them that it is in their best interest. It's just not your responsibility to make the decision for them and manipulate them into complying.

Let's say a sales prospect doesn't realize how much your *widget* will add to their life so you set out to persuade them. You do this through careful listening, questioning, understanding, and suggesting.

Afterward, the customer, having experienced the terrific results, is so very grateful for your patience and the time you invested in helping him that he becomes a huge referral source. Your work just got a whole lot easier because his referrals transfer his "know, like, and trust" feelings about you and his very positive feelings about your *widget*.

Again, good intentions are not enough. If you sense you are causing the other person to feel bad, guilty, or foolish, you most likely are manipulating. And unless you are saving someone from some clear and present danger to their lives, the end does *not* justify the means.

Stay attuned to your authentic core. It will guide you along the correct path. If you feel any of the negative emotions previously described while being manipulated, you will know you are veering off the path of persuasion and onto the road of manipulating another.

So persuasion, good; manipulation, bad. Just as we don't want to be manipulated by others, we must be sure we don't—even unintentionally—do it to someone else.

I guess we could say that, above all, our aim as positive persuaders and influencers is, at best, to help the other person as well as ourselves. At worst, it's to do no harm while we obtain what we need.

And, of course, in either case, helping the other person feel good about themselves and the situation is *always* the correct thing to do.

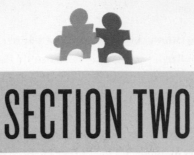

SECTION TWO

Control Your Own Emotions

This Comes Before Everything Else in the Process, Every Time

Self-Control is the very essence of character. To be able to look a man straight in the eye, calmly and deliberately, without the slightest ruffle of temper under extreme provocation, gives a sense of power which nothing else can give. To feel that you are always, not sometimes, master of yourself, gives a dignity and strength to character, buttresses it, supports it on every side, as nothing else can. This is the culmination of thought mastery.

—Orison Swett Marden, *Peace, Power & Plenty* (1909)

There was plenty of room to pull safely into the parking space. However, I was rushing and not paying attention, as I should have been, and I didn't notice the man coming out of the car parked in the very next space. I hit the brakes in plenty of time, but it gave the man a scare. He glared at me in a way that communicated he was *none too pleased*.

He *reacted*. Who could blame him? Now I had a choice: to react to his reaction, or to respond, thereby diffusing an otherwise uncomfortable (and potentially nasty) situation, and hopefully turning a potential enemy into a friend—an adversary into an ally. I chose to respond. I immediately raised my hand in a slight wave and, with a sincere smile, mouthed, "Sorry!"

The man then immediately responded with a smile and a wave of his own and said, "No problem." And when I got out of my car, he actually said, "Sorry, I should have looked before getting out of my car."

Can you believe that?! I'll never forget that incident. Not because it was so special, but because it's so common. It reminded me how simple and easy it really is to take what could be a mountain, and keep it a molehill.

And while every situation is different, the basic principle holds true: if you choose to control your emotions—to respond instead of to react—you can influence almost every interaction for the better.

In the process of becoming an Ultimate Influencer, controlling your emotions comes before every other step, every time.

In his book *Guard Your Anger*, Rabbi Moshe Goldberger writes, "God created oysters with the capacity to transform an irritating piece of sand into a pearl. This serves as a model for us—every trial contains precious jewels which we can find and develop."

Every encounter you have with an angry person, with someone who disagrees with you or criticizes you, and every frustrating challenge you face is an opportunity to create a better outcome—a pearl. And the first step in creating that pearl is to control yourself—the only part of the situation that is in your power to control.

In this section, you'll recognize the extreme importance of the Marden quote on the previous page. Mastering this trait of self-control will set you up for success in all your interactions. And you'll learn through many of the examples in this section exactly how you can very naturally and effectively accomplish this.

RESPONDING VERSUS REACTING

When dealing with any potential adversary, you will face the same choice again and again: whether to respond rationally to what is happening or react emotionally.

Though the words respond and react are similar, the difference between the two is quite significant. I still recall, on one of his audio programs more than twenty-five years ago, Zig Ziglar—in his distinctive and magnificent Southern drawl—asking, "Did you *respond well* to the medication your doctor prescribed, or did you have a *bad reaction*?" That describes the two ideas perfectly.

Yes, the *mighty person* controls his emotions rather than letting them control his behavior. This self-control is important and powerful not only in what it allows you to do but in who it allows you to be. Referring again to the Marden quote we saw earlier, knowing that you are always in control of yourself supports your character like nothing else can.

When you react, you are being controlled by outside circumstances, whether it be a difficult situation or person. When you respond, however, you are in control of yourself, of your emotions.

In other words, as my Dad says, "You're the boss of yourself." Then—and only then—are you in a position to take a potentially negative situation and turn it into something positive for you and everyone involved.

Short term, you'll find yourself much more comfortable and relaxed knowing that you can handle any potentially difficult situation that comes your way. You'll do so without being thrown off track, and you'll feel good about yourself having handled it correctly.

Long term, you'll have a true feeling, inside and out, of self-confidence for having handled countless situations that previously would have thrown you for a loop and perhaps upset your entire day.

Now, I can assure you from personal experience, this *doesn't* mean you won't mess up from time to time. But those times will be few and far between. And you'll always be aware of why it happened, which will help you adjust and course correct for the next time.

So how do you develop response consciousness? The same way you develop any other skill; you practice. First, set a goal for yourself to live in this type of consciousness. Then come up with a plan. For example:

1. Imagine situations where you'll have the opportunity to respond instead of react and see yourself doing it perfectly. Like an astronaut simulating a flight, this will serve as great practice.

2. Write the words "Respond vs. React" on yellow sticky notes and put them in places where you'll constantly see them: your phone, your computer, your bathroom mirror, et cetera.

3. Practice responding to normally difficult situations and people throughout the day, taking pleasure in your victories (victories over *yourself*!). Remember, each small success retrains your brain, allowing for continued success in future similar situations.

4. If you'd like, you can even keep score at the end of each day by grading yourself from one to ten (perfect). Don't get frustrated

with low beginning scores, but take great pleasure in seeing the scores get higher and higher every day. And they will.

You won't have to go through the visioning, sticky-note, and scoring process forever; only until you've reached a high enough level of proficiency. After that, only general awareness is required.

For many of us, myself certainly included, this is an ongoing journey.

It's also worth it. Very, very worth it!

EFFECTIVELY HANDLE
VERBAL ATTACKS

You pick up the phone and are immediately met with rage from the person on the other end. Yes, you're being verbally assaulted. And regardless of whether it is someone you know well or a complaining customer not happy with some aspect of their purchase, you don't handle it well.

You either shout back with words just as venomous as your adversary's or you passively take it; feeling afterward as if you've barely survived an explosion. Which, figuratively speaking, isn't too far from the truth.

Even while beginning to master turning adversaries into allies, it's common to be thrown off when verbally attacked. The reason is simply the surprise itself.

So how do you effectively handle it, diffuse it, and turn the situation 180 degrees?

Don't Be Surprised

Let's look at how to prepare for these attacks so the surprise factor will not be able to get the best of you. Then we'll go through some specific language you can use to effectively diffuse the situation and bring it under control. You'll have your adversary eating out of your hands.

Step 1. Be conscious that being verbally attacked will probably happen. I can't think of anyone it's never happened to.

Step 2. Mentally rehearse a situation in which, without any hint or warning, you are being verbally attacked. See yourself, in your mind's eye, responding (not reacting) with calmness, completely in control of your own emotions and thus in control of the situation.

If you can do it in your mind, you can do it in real life.

Just as an astronaut training for a mission goes through numerous simulations before ever actually going into space, you'll find that rehearsing the scenario in your mind puts you nine steps ahead of the game . . . in a ten-step game.

When It Actually Happens

What do you do when a customer, friend, coworker, or family member is in a bad mood and approaches you in an angry, challenging manner and unleashes a small verbal assault?

Step 3. Again, before anything else, *respond* by maintaining control of yourself and your emotions. Remain calm, take a deep breath, and actually hear the other person out. Interrupting will only *add* fuel to the fire. Display interest in what she is saying, but show no negative emotion.

Step 4. When she finally pauses, simply use these words: "I . . . might possibly owe you an apology. Did I say or do something to offend you?"

One of two types of responses will follow.

If it was nothing personal but she was simply in a bad mood, she will most likely grasp the inappropriateness of her actions. She will probably respond by saying something like, "No, I'm sorry, I'm just in a bad mood. I had a bad day."

Step 5. Now you can communicate empathy by saying, "I understand. I've had those myself. Is there anything I can do to help?"

Even if she feels she has a legitimate complaint with you, she'll then—realizing you're not the enemy and are willing to hear her out—be willing to continue the discussion with a much more polite and logic-based approach.

Either way, you've gone a long way toward taking that lemon, turning it into sweet lemonade, and, without question, turning a potential adversary into an ally.

When That's Not Enough

Usually it really is that easy. But not always. At times a person feels he has a legitimate gripe (and perhaps he does) and is not content with your response. He needs to get his point across and is being quite loud about it to boot.

In that case, despite the other person's raised voice, it's very important that you don't raise yours. In fact . . .

Step 6. Lower your voice.

Even if the conversation didn't begin with a verbal attack, sometimes it simply happens in the course of disagreement. When your discussion turns less than cordial, and voices are becoming louder with each exchange, it's tempting and natural to think that if you just yell a little louder than the other person, you'll be heard and they will have to concede your point.

Yeah . . . no.

First, the other person probably won't hear you any clearer than you are hearing him. And even if he does, he's not listening.

The key to being heard—as unlikely as it sounds—is to actually lower your voice.

Yes, when the volume is escalating, step back. Control your emotions. Calm yourself. Speak softly. The other person will pause to hear what you have to say and both of your attitudes will become more relaxed.

Now you can make your point and be heard (see page 65 on clarifying questions). And the other person will, most likely, lower his voice as well. Now you can hear each other. An instant win . . . for both of you.

The key to handling verbal attacks is staying *conscious* of the situation; in this case, knowing that emotions have taken over and reintroducing calmness and logic.

Now you'll be much more effective and productive both for yourself and for others. And handling verbal attacks will simply be one more area you've learned to master.

MAKE CALM
YOUR DEFAULT SETTING

People like, trust, respect, and are more likely to be influenced by those who have the ability to remain calm and thoughtful. We can all achieve this. We just may need to change our default setting.

In computer science, the default setting is a particular setting or value for a variable that is assigned automatically by an operating system and remains in effect unless canceled or overridden by the operator. (Example: Susan changed the default setting for the font in the word processing program.)

Your default setting is your natural response—or, more likely, your *reaction*—to a certain stimulus. Much like a computer we tend to act the way we've always acted or the way that is most natural to us.

When an uncomfortable situation occurs, what is your default setting? Do you get uptight, panicky, angry, nervous, or hyper? Do you yell or become aggressive? Act forceful? Do you do this unconsciously and realize only later you've overreacted, if you even realize it at all?

Or do you remain calm? Do you stay in control and rationally assess the situation? Do you automatically slow down to make sure you're considering everything carefully?

Your default setting to pressure situations is directly proportional to your ability to problem solve, to live in the solution, and to lead, whether a team, business, charity, family, et cetera. This is so important. Remember:

> Your default setting to pressure situations is directly proportional to your ability to problem solve, to live in the solution, and to lead.

The All-Important System Override

Good news: as operator of your own system, you can override your natural default setting. And you can help others do the same.

An excellent example of this is Lisa Wilber, a top Avon consultant (she's their fourth highest money earner in the country) and owner of the personal development company The Winner in You. One day she received a panicky phone call from one of her consultants who had a "catastrophic problem."

As you may have guessed from the quotation marks, the problem wasn't catastrophic at all. It was inconvenient, *not* catastrophic. But the consultant, congruent with her current default setting, reacted with panic. So when she called Lisa she was already upset and agitated.

Fortunately, Lisa's default setting is set on calmness and serenity so she simply walked her through the situation and together they came up with a solution.

She would not have been able to do that if her default hadn't been on the right setting, allowing her to first reframe the context for her consultant.

Is it always easy to handle what life throws at us? Of course not. However, generally speaking, any potential problems or challenges—whether you're leading other people or just yourself—will be easier to understand, deal with, figure out, and move past successfully when approached calmly.

But can you really actually *change* your default setting after living with it for so long?

Absolutely. Just follow these six steps to reset yourself for calm.

1. Decide you want to change and that from now on your default setting will be on calm.
2. Vividly imagine that the next time a potentially upsetting situation occurs, you become calm.
3. When the next such situation occurs, default to calm.
4. Forgive yourself if you slip up (we all do!).
5. When you do default to calm, take great pleasure in the fact that you did.
6. Know that since you did it once, you have the ability to do it every time.

The ability to remain calm when others aren't is another separator that creates influence and allows us to gently persuade. It's also a huge help when turning adversaries into allies. After all, as in the above example with Lisa, that rare person who stays calm controls not only themselves but the entire process. That's the great leader; the powerful influencer.

This reminds me of one of my favorite quotes from one of my favorite books, *As a Man Thinketh*, the timeless classic by James Allen published in 1915: "The more tranquil a man becomes, the greater his success, his influence, and his power for good. He is like a shade-giving tree in a thirsty land, or a sheltering rock in a storm."

And that's exactly what Lisa was for her team member, wasn't she?

Working Within *Their* Default Settings

Inspired years ago by a particular teaching in James Redfield's best-selling *The Celestine Prophecy*, I developed a concept I refer to as "personal dramas." These are emotional *reactions* we have when faced with stressful situations, including interpersonal confronta-

MAKE CALM YOUR DEFAULT SETTING | 41 |

tions. They are totally unconscious behaviors and—while not even aware we are displaying them—cause us to falsely believe we are in control of ourselves and the situation at hand.

I suspect we all have these to a certain degree. They manifest differently for different people: anger, panic, domination, victimhood, et cetera.

Understanding personal dramas led me to understand default settings.*

I began realizing, first in myself and then in others, the insidious tendency to default into personal dramas. Knowing that most people did not recognize this inclination, it made sense that arguments could occur and accelerate as a result.

It seemed I could increase my influence if I could both consciously reset my own default settings and work successfully within the default settings of others. Putting this into practice over the years I've found that, indeed, not only are pressure situations simpler to handle, but I can also much more easily turn potential adversaries into allies.

Yes, you can do this, too. There are only three steps.

1. If necessary, change your default setting (using the six steps we've already discussed).
2. Notice and understand *the other person's* default setting.
3. Handle his or her default setting appropriately.

Let's look at step three in action through some personal examples.

"Joe" has done private contract work for me for many years. Great guy. Terrific guy. And he's truly superb at his job. His only challenge—in my opinion—is his default setting.

When faced with a pressure situation, it's usually set to "I can't." In other words, when asked about a certain task, he immediately tells me it can't be done, that it's "impossible."

---

* That, and because my computer kept defaulting to 10-point Helvetica!

That's just Joe. It's the way he is . . . programmed. It doesn't change the fact that he's a good person or excellent at what he does. Or the fact that he has saved my rear end on numerous occasions.

Nor does it change the fact that whatever he is dealing with is not at all impossible, and he always comes through for me in the end!

Again, it's just his default setting. And rather than try and change him, I just work within that context. Because I now understand his default settng, I just wait it out. I tell him what I need and then wait for him to tell me that he can't, it won't work, it's impossible, et cetera. Then I wait a few more moments while he processes the information (and, yes, he does this every time), and then he tells me how he *can* do it. And he does.

In other words, Joe handles what he sees as stressful situations by first giving himself breathing room—he says it can't be done. When I used to immediately (and with frustration—*my* default setting) ask him why not, or say, "Of course it can! You've done it before," it would set him into panic and delay the solution. Instead, I let him go through his processing routine.

A Different Way for a Different Person

"Sue" is a longtime friend of mine. She considers me if not a mentor, then certainly a trusted sounding board when she's deciding what new direction to take. Sometimes, because we are close, I'll volunteer an idea without being asked.

Regardless of what I suggest, she immediately becomes anxious and says something like, "I don't think that would work for me," or, "I wouldn't feel comfortable doing that."

That's her default setting. So now, after I make the suggestion and before she responds, I quickly say, "Don't decide now. In fact, it might or might not be a good move for you. Think about it for a day or so in order to weigh the options."

The phrases "Don't decide now" and "Think about it for a day or so" are what I call an out or a back door. For people like Sue who have to work through all of the angles before accepting a new idea, having an emotional escape route helps them grow both more confident and more comfortable. They don't feel pressured. And they are more likely to carefully consider the options in a responsive rather than a reactive way.

The phrase "might or might not," also serves as an out, moving it from a directive to a choice, and provides the person with that same sort of comfort.

Using this method helps Sue make decisions based on her excellent sense of logic rather than on a reactive default setting.

Most people have a default setting, and they have a right to it, whether it serves them or not. And regardless of whether they are close friends or loved ones, coworkers, sales prospects, or a stranger you'll deal with only once, if it's important to influence them to your way of thinking, you need to acknowledge this and work effectively within *their* framework.

The more you can help them operate their default settings successfully, the better you can lead, persuade, and influence successfully, creating solution-based decisions and outcomes.

Rather than simply working successfully within their default setting, can you actually help them *change* theirs? Sure, but they must want to do so. If you have a relationship with that person where they are willing to let you help them, simply take them through the six steps we talked about earlier.

However, please know that you *cannot* do this during the time of conflict, when the default setting has been triggered. It must be done when they are not in an emotional state.

OVERCOME ANGER

Nobody can *make* you angry. You must give them permission to do so. They can, however, intentionally or unintentionally trigger your own reactive anger. And while it may be difficult, those who can avoid the anger-inducing influence of others are typically the most influential of all.

What does overcoming anger* have to do with Ultimate Influence? Practically everything. As we've discussed, a mighty person is one who can control their own emotions. This must take place before ever expecting to make that potential enemy our friend or turn that potential adversary into an ally.

Anger is a turnoff to people. You might be able to obtain *compliance* through displays of anger, but you will never get commitment.

Those who are wise and respected have an attitude of calm, and this elicits respect and trust from everyone around them.

---

* Please note that, for the sake of this discussion, I'm talking only about unhealthy anger. There is a time and place for legitimate anger—someone you love has been hurt; an injustice of some sort has occurred—and effectively channeling that for a positive outcome. Here we are discussing only the negative and counterproductive variety.

For many years I had a huge problem with anger. It was based on a combination of ego and lack of self-respect. Though I was a genuinely kind person, whenever I felt as though I'd been wronged, my ego took over and not only personalized it but focused intently on it.

My anger (along with my propensity to hold grudges) was a self-destroyer, and at a certain point I knew it had to end. Along with other areas in which I felt a particular character trait needed improvement, I began to work on my personal transformation. Fortunately, anger is no longer an issue, and most people who know me now would probably not suspect it ever was.

This has made a huge difference for me in terms of personal happiness as well as my ability to influence, persuade, and serve others. And it will do the same for you.

Keep in mind that because the cells that make up our body all take their signals from the mind, the physical effects of holding a grudge, or any type of unnecessary anger, are immense. Of course, none of this bothered the people I was mad at. By and large, they never knew. But considering I seethed with my intense dislike of them, they sure held a lot of power over me, didn't they? It reminds me of the famous quote attributed to Gandhi:

> Don't hold a grudge. It allows a person to live in your head rent-free.

Deciding not to hold a grudge, even against someone you feel deserves it, does not mean you accept their behavior. As we've all read, you don't forgive them—or let go of your grudge—for their sake, but for your own sake.

And not only can you not effectively influence someone against whom you hold a grudge, but the negative energy you emit to *everyone*—as a result of holding grudges against *anyone*—will make you less attractive, and thus a less powerful influencer than you otherwise could be.

Seven Steps to Overcoming Anger

If you're concerned that anger is so wired into your DNA that you cannot overcome it, let me assure you that's not the case. And once you do, you'll wonder why you ever allowed yourself to carry it for so long. You'll be forever glad you opted for inner peace. It'll be that dramatic a difference for you.

So let's look at the steps we can take in order to begin the transformation.

1. **Become aware.** Without awareness that there is a problem, we won't do what we need to do in order to overcome it. If you've recognized anger as a problem in your life and a hindrance to your personal and professional effectiveness, I congratulate you.

2. **Desire.** Truly desire to lose anger as a character trait. This is key. Without the desire to change and a commitment to see it through, utilizing these methods will be no more effective for the long term than trying to cover an already infected injury with a bandage.

3. **Imagine.** Picture situations and scenarios that could happen (perhaps based on past experience) that would elicit anger and see yourself handling them in a calm, constructive, and positive manner. As mentioned earlier, this is similar to an astronaut running simulated scenarios to prepare for her missions.

4. **Play.** That is, play a mind game. Pretend you are in the midst of an outburst of anger. Then imagine that a seven-foot-tall, 450-pound, ferocious-looking man wielding a machine gun enters the room, looks at you, and says, "If you don't stop your anger right now, you're in trouble." Would you be able to calm down and immediately end your angry outburst? I don't know about you, but I sure would, and fast!

5. **Recognize.** If you could do it in that situation, then you've just proved to yourself that you are capable of not becoming angry whenever you are motivated enough not to be. And if you can do it once, you can do it whenever you choose.

6. **Apply.** Next time you find yourself in a situation where anger is welling up and you feel as though you're going to explode, first become conscious of the situation. If you begin to rationalize that you can't stop yourself, imagine the very large machine-gun-wielding man threatening you. Remember that you could (and would!) calm yourself if you found yourself in that circumstance. And if you could do it then, you can do it now.

   Your desire to lose the trait of anger will have to be stronger than the immediate gratification of letting yourself explode into the familiar angry rage.

One more. And, this is vitally important:

7. **Build on your small successes.** You don't have to be 100 percent successful in order to take pleasure in your progress. Maybe the first few times you simply don't get as angry as usual. Or you handle it well a couple of times and then slip up. Then you do it well again. Don't put pressure on yourself to be perfect. Just do your best. You're well on your way.

Will the above steps simply keep you from exploding outwardly while actually maintaining the rage inside? Not if you don't want it to. You can help yourself along in the process by focusing on gratitude for all the good in your life. The more in tune you are with gratitude, the less you'll feel the need to be angry. If you have issues that need to be addressed before you can release your anger, professional counseling is always an excellent option, as well.

If your tendency is to react in anger, you'll always have to stay aware and conscious and continue to work on it. But if you're like me, you'll so love the new feeling you have that it'll be worth the effort. You'll realize that anger is usually a choice, and not a productive one. And, without it as a constant force, your life is much lighter and far more productive.

THE PERSUASIVE POWER OF POSITIVE DETACHMENT

I call it emotional posture—that great state where while you might *prefer* a certain result, you are not emotionally attached to it. In other words, yes, you care . . . but *not that much*. Sure, you'd *prefer* your desired result to take place, and if it does, that's terrific! However, your personal happiness, joy, and peace of mind are in no way dependent upon it.

Why is that so important? Because when you are detached from the outcome in a positive way, not only are you less bothered when you don't get what you want, the chances are better that you *will* get what you want. Not due to some mystical or magical reasons, but for very practical ones.

Without the attachment you are able to focus more clearly on your goal without the distraction of fear getting in the way (attachment is *always* accompanied by fear). Others, seeing your calm and confident manner, are more attracted to you and to your desired outcome, as well.

For example, let's say you are having a political discussion with someone who, while her current position is different from yours, is open to listening to and considering your views. If you are too emotionally attached to her agreeing with you, you will argue, cajole, and overtalk in order to *convince* her. You might even come across as condescending. This will most likely cause her to feel defensive—because her ego has been bruised—and hold on to her current position even more strongly. That's exactly how most people would react to being spoken to that way. And since that's how most political discussions go, it's easy to see why few change their position based on these discussions.

On the other hand, if you can approach with positive detachment you will speak calmly and respectfully. Because she understands that you respect her regardless of the outcome (i.e., whether or not she ends up agreeing with you), she doesn't feel the need to resist and retreat to her original position and will be more willing to hear you out. The less attached to the outcome you are, the more persuasive you will be.

Just repeating the words "Don't be attached, don't be attached, don't be attached" doesn't accomplish this. What *does* is constant, consistent, and thoughtful practice. It comes through understanding that all that happens is for the good. It's understanding that if, for some reason, a desire is not fulfilled, it wasn't supposed to be.

Please don't think I'm suggesting that you should be lackadaisical in your efforts or not give 100 percent because *if it's supposed to be, it will just happen.* Uh-uh, *that's* magical thinking.

Do your very best, with all the effort you can muster. Then, regardless of the result, you have peace of mind in knowing you gave it your all. Your actions are really all that you can control. And to the degree that you are able to master emotional posture, or positive detachment, that's the degree to which your abilities to influence and persuade will continue to grow.

THINK *BEFORE* YOU SPEAK

Have you ever *reacted* to someone's words or actions with a caustic, bitter, or even sarcastic remark, then immediately wished you could take it back? I know I have, and too many times to count. But you can't take it back! All you can do at that point is apologize and try to keep the conflict from getting even more out of hand.

My friend Paul Myers says that an angry word is like a bullet— once fired, you can't take it back. A good plan is to think *before* you speak. Be silent for a moment. For most of us, this does not come naturally. We must practice, imagine, and prepare ourselves in advance. Sometimes not saying anything at all (at least for a moment or two) is the smartest thing we can do.

Once you've had a chance to consider the situation, you can now, thoughts in hand, utilize the principles we're discussing throughout this book.

While it's best to handle a conflict before it ever takes root, if a conflict is about to occur, the next best thing you can do is to stop it before it escalates.

Often, at the point that someone criticizes, corrects, or otherwise insults you, you have a choice right then and there to *think* before you speak. Consider carefully, before you fire the verbal bullet that you can't take back.

Want to say the right thing? Want to frame a wise, gentle, problem-quelling response? Then give yourself a chance. Say nothing for a moment. You'll come out ahead.

The benefits of silence extend beyond face-to-face encounters.

I was reading a Facebook post from a friend of mine, a well-respected professional with an always kind and calm manner. It was interesting to see him admit to having, what he described as, "a very unproductive, unprofessional tantrum in the form of an email that grew very long."

Fortunately, before sending it, he had the wherewithal to run it past a friend of his who suggested he delete it rather than send it.

This brings up several different options we have when we are so angry that we just want to explode at someone via an email.

1. **Take the Abe Lincoln approach.** When the sixteenth U.S. president was angry at someone, he would write a scathing letter, seething with every negative invective that came to mind. He would then sign it, seal it, stamp it, and tear it up into so many tiny pieces there was no chance of it ever being seen by the culprit who elicited those feelings. Lincoln used this technique to flush his anger. He never intended to actually send the letter.

2. **Wait before sending.** I can't tell you how many times just waiting twenty-four hours before sending an email has saved me from hurting another person, causing huge (and perhaps irreparable) damage to a business or personal relationship, and embarrassment to myself.

   That twenty-four-hour delay will result in a much kinder, tactful, and more effective message. Or it might help you realize that the correct response is not to send the email at all.

3. **Enlist help.** Writing effective emails is something I consider to be a strength of mine. Still, before sending an email in the midst of

"ticked-off-edness," I will often run it past a trusted friend or advisor and ask for critique and help.

Those I ask know me well enough to know if this letter is the "rational me" or an "angry/emotional me." They will often suggest changing certain words or adding helpful phrases—the same ones I would suggest to someone else if I were taking an objective look rather than being in an emotional, agitated state.

I'm reminded of another powerful thought from Daniel Goleman's *Emotional Intelligence*:

> A key ability in impulse control is knowing the difference between feelings and actions, and learning to make better emotional decisions by first controlling the impulse to act, then identifying alternative actions and their consequences before acting.

Brilliant!

So write the email. But don't hit send. At least not yet! Not until you are first in control of your own emotions, understand the consequences of your actions, and utilize one of the above options.

AGREE TO DISAGREE

t can be one of the most emotionally trying experiences of all. The *adversary* in this case might be a business associate, a member of a charity organization you both belong to, or, most likely, a close friend or family member. You feel very, very strongly about a certain point or idea. So do they. Unfortunately your two beliefs are diametrically opposed. And it doesn't matter how well you've learned to utilize the principles and strategies in this book, they ain't gonna budge.

Indeed, sometimes you're just not going to successfully move a person to your side of an issue. And because the correct conclusion or point of view is so very obvious to you and something you feel strongly about, that disagreement can dig into your emotional storehouse and cause feelings of frustration, resentment, and anger. Yet, it is what it is.

Again, take, for example, a conversation about politics.

Despite the old admonishment not to discuss politics in polite company, it makes sense that if we believe something is important for our country, we are naturally going to want to persuade others to agree. And when approached correctly and the other person is open to the conversation, there is no reason not to have that discussion.

How you approach the persuasion process, however, is important. Whether in political debate or any other area of disagreement, you're much more likely to be successful when coming from a place of respect rather than anger and vitriol.

I personally find the back-and-forth arguments I observe on social media about politics—filled with personal, vicious, and hateful insults toward those who disagree with one another—extremely disappointing. I doubt that many opinions are ever actually changed, but I don't doubt that friendships (or potential friendships) are harmed and even lost.

Of course, even rational, respectful disagreement doesn't ensure persuasion. I believe the question then is not, *should* we talk about a certain topic, but, when should we *stop* talking about that topic?

I believe the answer is, when you and the other person have reached a crossroad, that point where any further discussion cannot possibly help your relationship, but might just hurt it. At that point it is best to respectfully agree to disagree. This honors the person's right to believe a certain way without you *agreeing* with that way.

One benefit is that it leaves people much more open to your other ideas when you speak again. And maybe you can even revisit the current idea at some future time. This could never happen without their trust that you will—in the end—respect their right to believe what they choose to believe.

Yes, because the person knows you will not try to coerce or bully him into accepting your opinion, he'll actually be more open to the possibility of embracing your opinion, should you be able to make your point persuasively enough.

So know what to say and how to say it. And also when to *stop* saying it.

CONSIDER THE SOURCE

As a leader, as an Ultimate Influencer, you'll receive criticism. It comes with the territory. And learning how to handle and grow from it is key to increasing that influence.

Back in college, I was heavily involved in school politics. Whether in school or the real world, anyone involved in the public sphere is subject to opinions that are not always complimentary. In those days, I was prone to taking this type of criticism personally. Very personally!

I'd often complain to my friends, Bruce and Joe, about this "unfair treatment."

At the time, Bruce was president of the college's Student Government Association and Joe was senate chair. One thing I really admired about them both was that they didn't seem to mind criticism directed toward them.

Whenever I'd moan about some criticism I'd received, Joe would simply say, "Bob, consider the source!" In other words, before getting upset, determine how much weight you should even give this person's opinion.

Actually, considering the source of the criticism is a good idea no matter the context. When receiving disturbing feedback, if the source has said similar things that were nonsensical or baseless, you can probably chalk it up to a pattern and not pay it a whole lot of attention. (Unless, of course, you think he or she has a valid point. This is one area of great maturity; controlling your emotions to the point that you can think clearly, without your ego getting in the way.)

On the other hand, if you know the source to be rational and clear thinking, and if you've previously agreed with this person on other occasions, it might be productive to give their critique some thoughtful attention. Not that you have to agree, but looking from their viewpoint might turn out to be very helpful.

Even when you take someone's criticism seriously, you do not need to take it personally. Those are two different concepts. And it is an excellent opportunity to practice controlling your emotions.

First, practice determining whether the criticism is worth taking seriously. If it is, act accordingly and be prepared to make changes. Second, practice not taking it personally, regardless of where it comes from.

Either way, consider the source.

SECTION THREE

Understand the Clash of Belief Systems
Avoiding Those Deadly Misunderstandings

The range of what we think and do is limited by what we fail to notice. And, because we fail to notice that we fail to notice, there is little we can do to change—until we notice how failing to notice shapes our thoughts and deeds.

—R. D. Laing (Scottish psychologist, 1927–1989)

What I believe you heard is not what you think I said.

—A. Nonymous

Some years ago a friend of mine was thinking about moving to my area and asked if a particular home he'd heard about was near the ocean. I said, "No, it's pretty far away," so he decided he wasn't interested. When he and his wife arrived for a visit, they asked me to show them the home just so they could see it. Upon viewing it he said, "I thought you told me it wasn't near the ocean!"

ME: "It isn't!"

HIM: "It is, too!"

ME: "No, it isn't!"

HIM: "Yes, it is!"

(No, neither of us stuck out our tongue at the other and went "Nyah, nyah.")

Let's analyze this. The truth is that that home was seven miles from the ocean. I, living in Jupiter, Florida, and two blocks from the ocean, feel that seven miles is far away. He, being from the Midwest, feels that seven *hundred* miles from the ocean isn't too far away.

Our miscommunication had to do with our belief systems. Why did neither of us think to mention the exact number of miles? Probably because we both assumed we shared the same point of view. This is the natural trap of belief systems.

A belief system is simply how we see our world. Unlike a *truth*, which is objective fact, our personal belief systems—the combination of upbringing, environment, and everything that has entered our minds since birth—is what colors that truth, providing us with our unique interpretation of the facts.

Our belief system, while beginning early, is actually rooted much further back.

From the moment human beings walked the earth, beliefs were a function of survival for individuals and the clans in which they lived. Fortunately, things have changed and life has become significantly easier.

So while it was necessary for our cave-person ancestors to know that a certain sound signaled either a potential dinner . . . or a potential *diner* (hence the importance of making major decisions based on limited information), such is no longer the case for us.

Nonetheless, we still make many decisions the same way.

Just because a certain belief is part of our belief system doesn't mean it is bad. A number of our beliefs are extremely valuable and serve us well.

The trouble occurs when we fail to *notice* our belief systems at work. Then we operate in accordance with all of our beliefs, even those that not only don't serve us but can cause us—and perhaps others—harm.

While the above story was perhaps somewhat amusing and relatively harmless, such is not always the case. All too often, feelings are hurt, work is improperly done, team members discouraged, and friendships questioned because both (or many) parties involved simply judged the other's meaning based on their *own* belief systems. Or they assumed their intended meaning was understood by the other(s).

We'll look at some specific examples of this all-too-common interpersonal challenge throughout the chapters in this section. The key to success in working within belief systems is the ongoing realization that they are always in play; they are always taking place, with every thought and within every word, conversation, and—yes— confrontation.

As the Irish playwright George Bernard Shaw said, "The Problem with communication is the illusion that it has occurred." As human beings we tend to believe that others think and feel as we think and feel. We are usually incorrect in that conclusion. People around us operate out of their own paradigm and worldview, and so do we. And without understanding this, we are stuck on the same level of misunderstanding and miscommunication as everyone else.

This is the truth and brilliance of the quote by R. D. Laing that led this section.

Really grasping this will not only make your life a whole lot more pleasant, it will provide you with a unique advantage: you'll be one of the few people who understands . . . that nobody really understands another human being.

In this section you will not only come to appreciate why this realization is so important, you'll also learn how to work within it in order to establish yourself as a person of great wisdom and Ultimate Influence.

BELIEF SYSTEMS—
THE PROBLEM AND THE SOLUTION

Why is it so often the case that what we're absolutely, positively sure we know . . . turns out to be wrong? Because as human beings, we make decisions and base our judgments on very limited information, which is controlled by our personal belief system.

In order to work effectively with belief systems, it's very important to understand the difference between a belief and a truth.

I define a *belief* as the truth *as one understands the truth* to be.

What exactly does that mean?

Truth itself *is* fact. On its own it is neutral, without feeling. It may be viewed as good or bad depending upon the context, situation, results, and people involved.

For example, the truth is, gravity works. You need not believe it in order for it to be true. It simply is a universal law, a truth! It manifests itself as good when it keeps you from floating thousands of feet into the air against your wishes. However, it could be interpreted as rather bad when falling out of a six-story building.

Viewing most interpersonal situations as good or bad, or even accurately, however, isn't always that easy because our belief system is so subjective.

Once formed, our basic beliefs are extremely difficult (though certainly not impossible) to change because they operate primarily on an unconscious level. And the unconscious rules. And it rules without most of us even being *aware* that it rules!

In other words, practically everyone makes pretty much every assumption and decision without even realizing *why* they're making it.

Not Aware of Not Being Aware

This is something that 99.9 percent of all the people you ever deal with or come across don't know. They are a virtual slave to a belief system that they had little to do with forming and don't even know they have. And, by and large, the same goes for us.

As previously mentioned, not all of our preprogrammed beliefs are harmful. But all too many of them are.

In his best-selling books, author Randy Gage details the process of how we get infected with "memes" or mind viruses, based upon having subconscious beliefs that are often limiting or negative—and we don't even realize they are there. And once you're infected with a mind virus, it can run your entire operating system.

At the very least, they affect the way we see the truth. At their worst, they cause you to sabotage your own success.

As Pindar, the mentor in John David Mann's and my book *The Go-Giver,* told his protégé, Joe, "Appearances can be deceiving. Truth is, they nearly always are."

The reason they are deceiving is because—as the saying goes—we don't view it as *it* is, we view it as *we* are. And we view it from the angle of our personal belief system.

Whether a person grows up the product of a loving relationship or a difficult or abusive relationship, they will most likely *believe* that is the *truth* about relationships.

Whether a person grows up being taught that money is evil and that the only way to become wealthy is by taking advantage of others, or that money is simply the result of providing great value to the lives of many others, he or she will most likely *believe* that this is the *truth* about money.

Whether a person grows up witnessing win/lose situations or that win/win is the highest value, he or she will most likely *believe* that this is the *truth* about dealing with others.

And since these are the truths they believe, they will unconsciously steer their way to their truths, according to their beliefs. Even if it is counterproductive to their personal happiness.

I'm sorry to hit you so hard with this; however, when you understand it, it suddenly makes a lot more sense why people do what they do, act as they act, and have the high number of interpersonal conflicts that they have.

The solution is simple—simple, *not* easy.

And that is, become aware. While you are learning about belief systems and the results they manifest, stay consciously aware. Notice that everything a person says or does (and that would include you) is a result of a certain belief. Then ask yourself, *Was that a conscious belief that drove that action or was it unconscious?*

As you begin to do this, watch the changes that take place in your life and in your ability to relate positively to others—and in your ability to influence and persuade others.

The Four Clarifying Questions

The next time you are in an interpersonal conflict or confrontation with someone, ask yourself these four questions:

1. How is my personal belief system distorting the actual truth of the situation?
2. How is his or her personal belief system distorting the actual truth of the situation?
3. What questions can I ask this person that will clarify my understanding of his version of the truth (his belief system)?

4. What information can I give that will help her clarify her understanding of my version of the truth (my belief system)?

As the saying goes, within conflict between you and another person, there are generally three truths: your truth, the other person's truth, and the *actual* truth (really, those first two *truths* are just *beliefs*).

Through questions, as well as a caring exchange of information, you can discover the real truth, generating understanding, respect, peace, and trust.

13

"HOW WOULD YOU DEFINE . . . ?"

A Rabbi teaching a lesson on thought processes asked who would be offended if approached by someone who called them a "bafoostick." Some members of the class raised their hands and some did not. Finally, one asked the Rabbi if he would be offended if that happened to him.

"I don't know," replied the Rabbi. "But the first thing I'd do is ask, 'What is a bafoostick?'"

Often the simplest of misunderstandings are the ones that cause the most confusion. In becoming aware of the belief systems at play in every situation you may be tempted to go straight for the tough stuff—deep desires, unspoken fears. But your first step should be to check your terms. Yes, misunderstandings can occur because of specific words and how different people define them.

Making things even more difficult is when the parties involved don't know that they are defining the word differently. In other words, since you both believe you are talking about the same thing, you might not even know what you're disagreeing about.

For example, Dave, with urgency in his voice, says to his project partner, "Margaret, we've got to get these proposals in *soon*, so let's plan accordingly." Margaret agrees. So she stays several hours later than usual to do her share of the work, only to find the next day that Dave is no closer to completing his part.

"Dave," she seethes, "I thought you said we have to get these proposals in soon. I passed up on taking my son to the ball game last night to get these done on time."

"When I said 'soon,'" says Dave sheepishly, "I meant within the next week or so."

Two dynamics were at work here. One is what we've been referring to as belief systems. Because, based on our past experiences, we believe something—in this case, the word soon—to have a certain meaning and we expect everyone else to as well.

The other is simply the fact that words do have different meanings and words such as soon are conceptual in nature. Combine these two dynamics and it is a recipe for disaster.

So, what to do?

Look out for words or ideas that are subjective—soon, often, later, nearby, long—and make a habit of asking, "How would you define . . . ?" whatever it is. You could also ask, "What do you mean by . . . ?"

For example, Margaret suggests to Dave that the proposal should be brief. Dave would be well served to ask, "Just for my own clarification, how would you define brief?" Now Margaret can explain that the word brief means two pages in this particular instance.

You can use this method for practically anything. Of course, the *way* we ask has much to do with its effect and acceptance. Obviously, the question must be asked and communicated in a way that elicits good feelings in the other person and not a sense of defensiveness, as though their motives are being questioned.

Yes, define your terms and ask others for their definitions, as well. This is a very effective way to keep misunderstandings from ever taking place.

14

ACCEPT THE RESPONSIBILITY FOR COMMUNICATION

I n *The Seven Habits of Highly Effective People*, Dr. Stephen Covey cited Habit Number Five as "Seek first to understand, then to be understood." Excellent advice.

That one idea, when followed, will make everyone's relationships much more, well, effective.

Let's take this now iconic teaching of Dr. Covey's and apply it, making sure we also take the next appropriate and vital step.

Once you understand the other person, it is equally important to make certain that you communicate your point so that the other person understands you and what you mean to say.

Thus, when it comes to effective communication, the onus is always on *us* to be sure the other person understands our point, want, or need.

I'll be forever grateful to one of my early mentors who told me:

When the shooter misses the target, it ain't the target's fault.

As much as we sometimes (only sometimes) wish that people could read our minds, they can't. And since we come from different places carrying different belief systems, the chances of their knowing exactly what we mean without our clarifying it are very slim.

And we cannot expect others to put that burden of understanding on themselves. If we do, we'll be disappointed.

So if our goal is to be the most effective and powerful influencer we can be, we must accept that responsibility.

One surefire way of successfully taking responsibility for hitting the communication target is to avoid giving—or accepting—mixed messages. These are deadly when it comes to effective communication.

One common type of mixed message is when a person says one thing, but follows it up with the opposite. For example, you say to your employee, "Al, I need the specs by this Friday, but don't rush if it's going to mean a substandard job."

Well, what exactly does this mean? Is Friday the deadline, or is excellence the top priority? What if, for whatever reason, both deadline and top quality are not possible? If Al doesn't know enough to ask for clarification, you might receive specs that are too late to present to your prospect or not up to quality standard. Don't depend on Al to read your mind and intuitively understand. He's the *target*. And if you don't hit the target, it won't be *his* fault.

Another type of mixed message is when you say one thing but your tone or body language says another. While you're saying, "No problem, I don't mind," your voice sounds defensive, your lips look glued to your teeth, and your body posture is tight as a drum. That is a mixed message.

This works both ways, of course, and though you shouldn't expect others to sort out your mixed messages, you *should* make a habit of clarifying others'. Asking some simple questions up front will save you a lot of potential confusion and complication later on.

You can ensure you don't fall victim to someone *else's* mixed message simply by—once again—putting the onus of clarification on yourself. This is easiest when using an "I message."

For example, imagine your boss tells you, "I definitely need the specs by this Friday, but don't rush if it's going to mean a substandard job."

You can say, "Mary, just for my own clarification, as I want to make sure to deliver the specs in the way you want them delivered, is it more important to you that . . . ?" and complete the question.

You crafted an "I message" by stating it was for your ("my") clarification and that you ("I") want to deliver the specs according to her needs. I messages are another excellent way to communicate a point with tact and ensure that the person does not go into defensive mode.

Now, if one of the two—quality or delivery date—is in fact more important to your boss, she can clarify right now, both for herself and for you. A misunderstanding is far less likely to ever have the opportunity to occur.

Yes, not only is it our responsibility to be certain our message is understood by the recipient, it's just as important to be sure we understand *their* message, as well.

And there's nothing "mixed" about that.

THE IMPORTANCE
OF CONSCIOUS AWARENESS

As we've established, our belief systems control us without our even being aware they are doing so. And that's the killer. We're not aware . . . that we're not aware. We're unconscious of the fact that we are acting out of a state of unconsciousness.

A good start to overcoming this challenge is to operate from a state of conscious awareness. You might even say that, ultimately, your influence is dependent upon your being consciously aware. And here's an excellent exercise with which to begin this journey.

Starting now, whenever you disagree with someone, or feel offended by something they've said or an action they've taken, be aware that two different belief systems—perhaps two extremely different and conflicting belief systems—are now operating.

Then realize that you are most likely making a decision—and possibly a major one—about this person and his or her words or actions, based on very limited information.

That will be a major step in remaining calm, helping you discover and deal with the *real* issue and determine how to deal with this person in a mutually beneficial manner.

Ask yourself two questions: *Are my feelings being filtered through my paradigm? Am I making a decision about that person based on limited information?*

The answer to both is probably yes, but as long as you are aware of that, you can adjust your thinking to be much clearer and your response much more productive, influential, and persuasive.

As entrepreneur and best-selling author T. Harv Eker says, "When you are consciously aware, you can think and act out of strength and choice as opposed to unconsciously accepted programming."

PERSONAL OR NOT?
HOW DO YOU KNOW?

Y ou come face-to-face with a person who is entering the building at the exact time that you are exiting. Making eye contact and even holding the door open that extra second for him, you smile graciously and say hello. Nothing. Or was that a soft grunt you heard? And if that was a grunt, was it a grunt of acknowledgment or a grunt of "Don't bother me"?

And, you wonder, if it was a "Don't bother me" grunt, who is he to grunt at me? What did I do to him that gives him the right to act so rudely to me?

Ever play those games with yourself? Not a very fun game, is it? You took something personally that most likely was not personal at all. There are a variety of possible reasons why he didn't acknowledge you.

He could have been in deep thought about a family challenge.

He could have just come from the hospital and is thinking about the sick friend he'd just visited.

He's about to be foreclosed upon and was in deep thought about his options.

He is late for a meeting and engrossed in how he is going to explain himself to his customer.

He's just not the type who greets or acknowledges strangers. (In other words, he operates under a different belief system than you do.)

Whether or not you feel he should still have acknowledged you (of course, that's based on *your* belief system, not his), you now know that his lack of response had nothing to do with you and everything to do with him. It was nothing personal.

Have you ever misjudged someone's intent and later found out you were wrong? I sure have.

Has someone ever done that to you? They have to me.

It's all about belief systems.

Want to be a hugely successful influencer? Judge favorably. Give people the benefit of the doubt. I'm not suggesting you be naive. I'm saying that if you don't know either way—and you probably don't—it will serve you much better to judge the other person favorably. If you don't have any reason to engage them, at least you'll simply feel better. If they are someone you know and need to work with, this practice will help you start with a positive rather than a negative frame.

Judging favorably hurts no one, helps everyone, and simply makes a lot more sense.

This is all easy to say. However, the problem of taking things personally is a plague for many people. It was for me for a long time, so I'm especially empathetic to those who suffer from this.

A blog reader asked: "Bob, how do you know if someone is trying to hurt your feelings or you're just taking something the wrong way?"

This is a question I'm sure most of us have had at some time in our lives. And depending upon the situation, it can actually be quite debilitating. As human beings, we certainly don't want to feel that anyone—whether stranger or close friend or family member—would ever want to intentionally hurt us.

However, in terms of the blog reader's question, I'm not sure there is a correct answer.

Much of what we take personally simply isn't personal at all. It's much more the result of our transferring our belief system onto others. In other words, since *we* think a certain way, we assume *they* do as well (i.e., their saying *this* could only mean *that*). And that is usually far from true.

Don Miguel Ruiz offers an excellent explanation of this phenomenon in his classic *The Four Agreements*. Two of his four "agreements" are, "Don't make assumptions" and "Don't take things personally." We all do these two things continuously.

There are questions you can ask yourself that, using logic, will indeed help you better determine that person's intent. But even then, be very careful to make sure you don't assume *your* logic/beliefs/agreements are *his* logic/beliefs/agreements.

Set the Question's Frame with an "I Message"

Let's say you want to discover the intent behind something your coworker or a friend or family member said. What's the best way to determine if it was or was not personal? Ask them with tact, and, if possible, using an "I message."

For example, rather than, "What *you* said made me feel badly. *You* really hurt my feelings, was that supposed to be a personal insult?" which puts the onus on them, you might say, "*I* felt really hurt by something that was said and, I've got to admit, I took it personally. Just for *my* own clarification, *I'd* like to ask you about it, if you wouldn't mind."

During my many years of living in anger, I often took things personally that, looking back on it, were most likely not personal at all. The vast amount of time I wasted and the energy I spent by letting this control much of my life was so very unnecessary.

So is someone trying to hurt your feelings? Or are you simply taking what they're saying the wrong way?

I don't know for sure, but the chances are excellent that it was nothing personal. After all, most people are far too busy thinking of themselves to be thinking about hurting you.

And maybe that's not such a bad thing to keep in mind.

LOVE LANGUAGES FROM
LIBERTY THE CAT

A while back, I posted the following on Facebook: "My stray cat, Liberty, left a mouse's head on the patio for me this morning. Not a dead mouse, the head of a dead mouse! I think that cat has been watching too many movies lately. Hmm, what is she trying to tell me?"

Although at the time I knew very little about cats (while I love all animals, for most of my life I've had only dogs), I was aware that they show appreciation to their humans by bringing them dead stuff. What was so amusing to me was that the mouse head reminded me of the horse's head from *The Godfather*—a symbol that sends an extremely powerful message.

Now, as opposed to the three or four responses I typically receive when posting something I feel is quasi-profound, this one brought more than seventy responses, many of which offered excellent suggestions.

Several people talked about seeing value from the other's point of view. Yes, while the mouse's head held no intrinsic (or, for that matter, extrinsic, or, for that matter, any!) value to me, it did for Liberty. Because she valued it, a friend suggested that I should at least value the thought, if not the gift itself. And in that sense, I would be valuing the gift.

A couple of people took the lesson that we should be careful to choose the gifts we give to others based on how *they* might value it. A great lesson, though I'm not sure Liberty will come around to it . . .

Here's a Terrific Book!

Both excellent lessons reminded me of a book I read many years ago by Dr. Gary Chapman entitled *The Five Love Languages*. He proposes there are five ways we receive love. They are: "words of affirmation," "quality time," "receiving gifts," "acts of service," and "physical touch." While most of us use all five Love Languages to a certain extent, usually one is primary and much more dominant than the others.

Here's the rub: in the same way that we as human beings tend to assume *our* belief system is just like everyone else's, we also tend to believe that the way we like to give and receive love is the same as another person's, even if we don't know anything about Love Languages.

Thus, if one partner's Love Language is acts of service and the other's is physical touch, the first person wonders why her thoughtful acts of service are never appreciated. She may not understand why the other person doesn't think of providing acts of service to her.

The fact that this is taking place on an unconscious level means that not only are the two people not speaking the same language, they don't even *know* they are not speaking the same language or that there *is even* a language to be spoken!

The basic Love Language principles taught by Dr. Chapman are not only for couples but—as suggested by his many additional books on the topic—for anyone. So from this moment on, after determining your Love Language as well as the other person's, be sure to stay conscious of both.

Or you could just adopt a stray cat. But watch out for those mouse heads. Your feline might be a member of the *Catra Nostra*.

FIRST, KNOW THE ISSUE.
THEN, CHOOSE THE WORDS

I often receive questions on my blog from those in challenging situations asking for help influencing or persuading another. They are frequently looking for the *exact words* that will suddenly turn their adversary into their ally.

Indeed, utilizing the right words and phrases is important. However, more often than not, these are simply the result of first *understanding the underlying cause* of the other person's position.

Correctly understanding the context—the other person's belief system—is critical in choosing the most persuasive words.

One reader was in the midst of a very challenging and upsetting situation and asked for an effective way to handle it.

> Dear Bob, the organization I belong to used to send plants and flowers to members who were ill. Although the money is there to continue doing this, they have decided to stop. I have been invited to the next board meeting to tell them why we should keep this very important practice going. I am at a loss of the proper words to say. Can you help me?

I suggested that while there is not necessarily one right way to say something, there are two things she could do to find the right way to approach this issue with the board.

1. **Discover why they feel this way.** What are their reasons, individually and as a group? Unless you know their reasons, you are flying blind. You have no idea whether or not your thoughts address their concerns.

   Just ask. Contact them individually and tactfully let them know you are interested in understanding more about their specific concerns. Be sure to frame these conversations as a discussion between allies, not adversaries.

2. **Honor their concerns.** Prepare your presentation in a way that honors them, their egos, and their intent. Chances are excellent that their intentions are based on what they believe is good for the organization. So when you begin by acknowledging that, it is a framing that continues to place you all on the same side, all wishing to benefit the organization and its members.

It's always important to understand that when approaching any type of similar situation, the first thing you must do is determine the underlying issue or issues. Otherwise you might use the most powerful words and persuasive phrases in the English language, and yet they will have absolutely no effect. Once you know the context, however, you can match the benefits of your solution with their wants, needs, and desires.

It's the same whenever you are dealing with anyone: friend, family member, coworker, boss, employee, sales prospect, whomever. It's only after you first see it from *their* point of view that you will be in a position to gear your words for both their benefit and for yours.

THE ANSWER?
BASED ON WHAT INFORMATION?

As an Ultimate Influencer, you'll often be asked for your opinion. Someone will explain a situation or tell you about an incident, perhaps one involving another person. Or they'll relate a scenario and ask what you would advise them to do.

It's important to understand that unless you have enough specific information upon which to offer an opinion, it is nothing more than quasi-educated guesswork. And when people's personal happiness or financial health is at stake, guessing isn't the correct way to approach it.

You see, when someone asks for our advice or an opinion, we tend to base our response on how *we* view the world (our own assumptions caused by and based on our own belief systems). So not only are we providing an answer that would serve us based on *our* values and beliefs, we are also very likely filling in the blanks with additional information not offered, which—according to our paradigm or world model—completes the story as we would understand it. Both are very dangerous.

If we are in a coaching or mentoring situation, this can manifest itself as a reflection of the coach or mentor himself or herself and not about the person or persons involved in the transaction.

Before we can helpfully respond, we must first ask helpful questions with the primary purpose of exposing all of our assumptions that will get in the way of truth.

It is very natural and easy to fall into the trap of answering questions even though we don't have enough information to go on. Ultimate Influencers don't do that.

CHAPTER

PERCEPTUAL REALITIES
EQUAL DIFFERENT CONCLUSIONS

One of my all-time favorite examples of how belief systems hinder communication is the East Indian parable about the six blind men and the elephant. Each of them touched a different part of the elephant's body and, naturally, based on their limited, individual viewpoints they came to six different conclusions about the essence of said pachyderm.

The nineteenth-century English poet John Godfrey Saxe, in his retelling of the story, relates that the man who felt the broadside proclaimed the elephant to be like a wall. The one feeling the tusk disagreed heartily, saying the elephant was like a spear. The third, feeling the trunk, thought they were both crazy and said an elephant is obviously like a snake. The other three, of course, from their points of view, had their own opinions.

In *Magical Worlds of the Wizard of Ads*, Roy H. Williams tells us that, "In *perceptual reality*, each of the men was correct." According to the author: "Most efforts at human persuasion are little more than one blind man urging another blind man to 'see' the elephant as he does."

I've rarely read a more brilliant, and more accurate, statement. It's a perfect summation of perhaps the biggest cause of ineffective influence and persuasion.

Not only do we see the world from our own set of beliefs but we assume that everyone else sees the world the same exact way!

Mr. Williams continues, "Have you ever paused to consider that your family, your friends, your co-workers, and your customers live in their own private, perceptual realities? Instead of expecting them all to see the elephant as you do, why not try to see what they're seeing? If you're patient, you will eventually see enough of the elephant from different perspectives to finally make sense of it all.

"And then," he concludes, "you'll have something to say that will really be worth hearing."

Wow, this is a great point. And we must—we absolutely *must*—see the reality based on *their* perception if we are going to obtain buy-in to our suggestions and ideas.

Constantly practice "seeing the elephant" from the other's point of view. Will it be easy? No, but it will result in learning a lot about the other person and his belief system, not to mention a lot about ourselves and *our* belief system, even those things that might keep us from being as effective as we can be.

CHANGE YOUR NON-SERVING BELIEFS TO BE MORE PRODUCTIVE

So are we as human beings victims of our belief systems? To a certain point, yes.

However, once you are consciously aware that your belief system drives your reactions or responses, you will be in a position to change that system in a way that will serve you much better.

And that's great to know, isn't it? It means that you genuinely have control over your life and the way you live it every day. And that even when a distressing or life-altering event occurs, you still have the ability, within your new and developed belief system, to respond in a more beneficial and productive manner.

On the other hand, trying to change *another's* basic belief system is not quite as doable. The good news is: you don't need to do so to be successful or influential. You only need to understand that they are operating from their own belief system. Then, utilizing the information in this book, work *within* their belief system in order to influence them in a way that benefits all concerned.

SECTION FOUR

Acknowledge Their Ego

Working Effectively Within the Ultimate Human Motivator

> I believe that the biggest problem that humanity faces is an ego sensitivity to finding out whether one is right or wrong and identifying what one's strengths and weaknesses are.
>
> —Ray Dalio, American businessman

T he majestic horse is strong and powerful, but it can also be wild. If the rider is in control of the horse, its power can be utilized to accomplish great things. On the other hand, if the horse is out of control, it can wreak all sorts of havoc, becoming a danger to itself, the rider, and everyone in their path. The ego is like the horse. We are its rider.

So long as we can control our egos (and their correlated emotions), there's a good chance we can help our potential adversary to control theirs. At that point, potentially horrendous situations can be turned into mutually beneficial results where everyone comes away much better off.

Ever notice that whenever the ego is mentioned in conversation, it is typically cast in a negative light? "She has such a huge ego," or "Wow, his ego is just totally out of control!"

Much of today's popular teaching dismisses the benefit of ego, relegating it to a nuisance that should be at least, ignored, and at best, obliterated.

Yet without the ego, nothing exceptional could ever happen. After all, if individuals are not aware of their existence or individuality and have no desire to improve their lot, what motivates them to increase the good in their lives? And if they are not increasing the good in their lives, they can't increase the good in anyone else's, either.

Yes, inventions are made, businesses are launched, diseases are cured, houses are built, and every modern convenience we have has emerged because of the ego.

Control the ego; master the ego, have your ego and the feelings that come with it working for you, and you can achieve beyond your wildest dreams.

The trouble appears when that part of the ego with unhealthy desires *controls us*. And what is far more difficult for us and for others, and what makes us far less effective than we could potentially be, is when we are not *aware* of this.

There is good reason why this aspect of the ego gets so much attention. It causes a whole lot of trouble and wreaks a whole lot of havoc in this world of ours. It's what compels well-meaning advocates to turn into despotic leaders. And it causes us to lose ourselves in very destructive patterns.

Anger, grudges, becoming easily offended, that's all about ego. And you can bet that the person you are trying to influence has *his* own ego monsters.

So while they may have the ability to provide you with what you want or need, if you're not conscious of their ego, it could very well spoil a workable solution. Be aware. Be careful. Acknowledge their ego and constantly keep it in mind.

As with belief systems, the onus is on you, the Ultimate Influencer, to work within their ego. They're not thinking of theirs, they're not thinking of yours. And chances are, even if they *were* aware of your ego, it wouldn't trump their own.

And that's okay, because Ultimate Influencers work within the context of a world that *is,* not necessarily one they wish it were. Though by doing this, we make the world a lot better and more functional for all concerned.

Keep in mind: whenever interacting with anyone—especially a potential adversary—be conscious of two egos between you. And remember, you are most likely the *only* one of the two who is conscious of either. So the onus is once again on you.

In this section, you'll learn exactly how—by keeping the other person's ego in mind—you can consistently use this often-uncontrolled driver to everyone's advantage, and turn even the most difficult potential adversary into your faithful ally.

DON'T SHAME OR EMBARRASS

T he Sages wrote, "It is better to jump into a flaming furnace than to embarrass somebody." Sounds a bit extreme, and maybe it is. On the other hand, maybe it isn't.

Of course, the message was certainly not to be taken literally, but to serve as a very pointed reminder that shaming or embarrassing another human being is something to avoid at practically all costs. Not only is it an unkind thing to do, but if you want any chance of positively influencing a person, shaming them will totally sabotage it.

I've personally never seen anything good come out of embarrassing someone. Never heard a joke so funny that it was okay that it came at the expense of another's feelings. Never seen an employee make a mistake that could be effectively corrected by the use of shame. Or a lesson to a child so profound that it was worth embarrassing or shaming him or her, especially in front of others.

It's a leadership and management maxim (and for good reason) to applaud publicly and criticize privately. When the young assistant does his job well, make sure to verbally acknowledge him in front of as many people as possible.

On the other hand, when he errs on an email or accidentally shares an incorrect piece of information with someone, call him aside and explain what was wrong and why, and how it can be done correctly the next time. Calling him out in front of everyone doesn't help anyone and could possibly discourage him, and make others afraid. When people operate in fear, they will comply but not commit.

Ultimate Influencers always carry an awareness, and act with that awareness, that a person's ego is the most fragile thing they have. And, unless the situation is extraordinary, would never purposely shame or embarrass another.

As Les Giblin, author of *How to Have Confidence and Power in Dealing with People,* wrote, "What counts is attaining personal satisfaction without trampling on the ego of the other person."

Ultimate Influencers know that when we get our point across in a way that leaves the other person's ego intact (via tact, empathy, and kindness), we earn their respect. We also earn their loyalty, commitment, and a willingness to more readily accept our point of view the next time a similar situation arises.

Don't Be Right at Someone Else's Expense

Related to this is publicly correcting another person in order to make your point. While the idea isn't to shame . . . the effect comes close. Embarrassing them or even just annoying them is not an effective way to create an ally now or for the future.

I remember all too vividly the jolt I received even though it was so many years ago. I was reading Dale Carnegie's timeless classic *How to Win Friends and Influence People* for the very first time and read this story he told about himself.

While at a banquet, Mr. Carnegie corrected a statement made by another guest about something trivial. Dale's friend, sitting next to him, overrode his correction, stating that the person was actually correct.

Later, when Dale asked his friend—whom he was certain knew better—why he did that, he received an admonishment. Paraphrased, it was, Why prove to someone that they are wrong? Why not let him save face?

It jolted me because I often did that very same thing. It was as though I couldn't resist pointing out someone's error, thereby highlighting my superior knowledge, even if it was harmless and trivial. And while no good was ever accomplished, it embarrassed the other person and caused resentment toward me.

Now, you might be thinking, *But, Bob, isn't it okay to correct when you know something is factually incorrect?* I would say that it depends upon the context of the situation. For example, is it important enough that it *needs* to be corrected? Is there a benefit to doing so, especially in front of others? Would it be more helpful or harmful to do so? Will it shame the person or be well received?

Let's say someone says, "Ted Williams was the best. Last guy to hit .406. Way back in nineteen forty."

The truth is that it was in 1941. Whether to correct the person or not depends upon the above questions. If it's a discussion between two friends, of course that's fine. Correct away. If not, and/or it would embarrass them publicly, don't. Should you tell them later? It depends. There is probably no harm in doing so. You could even use a lead-in phrase such as, "I might be wrong about this," and continue with, "I'm thinking it might have been in forty-one."

If he or she really cares enough to know the truth, they will check.

Yes, this is a very minor example, to be sure. Yet how often have you seen people correct others publicly as described above, doing more harm than good? Have you ever done that? Has someone ever done that to you? How did you feel about it, and about them?

Remember, a huge, huge part of influence—of obtaining commitment—is that the person likes you and trusts you. If you shame or embarrass them, does it seem they would be more inclined or less inclined to like you? And if they are in fear of being embarrassed by you, does it seem as though they are more likely or less likely to trust you?

Again, each situation is different. But when in doubt, it is best that if you're going to be right, that it *not* be at someone else's expense.

If You Have to Say "Just Kidding," It Probably Wasn't Funny

This final concept is without a doubt related to the above two. This one is probably the most insidious of all because while so many people embrace this behavior and feel it makes them popular, it is one of the most enemy-creating forms of communication there is— insulting others as a way of joking with them.

I once worked with a man named Dave whose favorite kind of humor was to "kiddingly" insult people. In most cases, it went like this: he insulted the person. They didn't laugh. He explained, "I'm just joking," and they chuckled begrudgingly. He thought it all worked out fine.

They didn't like him.

At one point, I took him aside and said, "Dave, if you have to explain to someone that you were 'just joking,' then there's a really good chance it wasn't funny in the first place."

Dave never really got it. Some people don't.

Benjamin Franklin, in his famous *Poor Richard's Almanack,* wrote, "Thou canst not joke an Enemy into a Friend; but thou may'st a Friend into an Enemy."

If you have to insult someone to be funny, it's probably best not to be funny. Yet, if *anyone* is to be insulted or poked fun at, it should be ourselves.

Come to think of it: why did we love Rodney Dangerfield so much? Aside from his brilliance, perhaps we loved him because he was always the target of his own jokes, which was disarming and allowed his audience to laugh along with him.

BE A JUDGE, NOT A LAWYER

The Sages said, "Be a judge, not a lawyer."

On the surface and when directed at an actual judge, the advice is obvious. Whereas a lawyer is paid to win the case for his or her client by any legal and ethical means possible, a judge is not. A judge's job is to ensure that the proceedings run smoothly, legally, and that both sides receive a fair hearing.

Thus a judge needs to understand both sides of the issue and be as impartial as possible.

Even if you don't wear a robe to work, this is sound advice. Have you ever been in a disagreement and so intent on winning your case that you kept trying to make your point even after realizing the other person was clearly in the right? I know I have. Unless you really are a lawyer, you might want to reconsider and take a different path. (And if you are a lawyer, be that way only in court!)

Here's a very difficult but very mature action to take—and if you can do this consistently, both the amount of respect you attain and your level of influence will skyrocket. Look at a disagreement as though you are a wise judge. In order to do this, you must step back from the situation and see both sides of the issue, yours *and* theirs.

Focus *especially* on theirs since you are predisposed to see your side. Ask yourself how you would judge this if you were an impartial juror.

Human that we are, being impartial is difficult when the ego wants to win at all costs—even if you're wrong. But the best way to overcome this unproductive desire is to practice being a judge.

Yes, control the inclinations of your ego. The result will be not only a better understanding of the actual situation but respect from the other person, as well. And when you communicate your final opinion, you are much more likely to be listened to. You've earned the right to be an Ultimate Influencer in their mind.

THE PRINCIPLE OF AGREEMENT

Dale Carnegie eloquently taught that there is no winning an argument. It makes sense, doesn't it?

After all, if you lose on merit, you've lost. However, even if you win on merit (showing the other person that you are right and they are wrong), you most likely still won't move the other person to take the action you desire. Why? Because you've insulted that all-important, emotion-based, decision-making instrument indigenous to the human being—the ego.

When that is the case, though you may be able to convince, rarely will you influence or persuade.

So what do you do when the other person says something you know is wrong? Well, agree. At first, anyway. This can be a wonderful way to disarm the person who, most likely, expects you to argue. But you aren't doing that. You are agreeing. And this leads to what I call the Principle of Agreement, and that is . . .

Nobody argues with himself (or herself).

Think about it. After agreeing with someone, will he or she ever respond by defiantly saying, "No, you're wrong, I was . . . wrong!"? I think not.

But don't stop there! Voicing your agreement does not imply that you should capitulate. Not at all!

Now you'll transition into some of the other methods of persuasion we've discussed and will continue to look at. A couple of good *buffers* or lead-in phrases you can use are, "I'm wondering if," or "Here's what I'm thinking," and then make your suggestion.

Notice I didn't say *but* because in this case it would negate your agreement. As an aside, while it's been said that it's always better to replace *but* with *and,* I don't think that is necessarily true. It's more politically correct than it is successful. Mainly because *and* doesn't always adequately make for the correct transition. Sometimes *but* is appropriate.

Often, simply pausing for a moment and then using a lead-in phrase is sufficient.

The key is, you've tactfully and effectively brought down the other person's defenses and made them much more amenable to your about-to-be-expressed point of view.

Persuasion is now well within reach.

Let's look at just one very quick example.

FRONT DESK AGENT: "It's hotel policy that we don't allow guests to check in until three p.m."

YOU: "Absolutely. It's very important to follow policy. It's there for a reason."

You didn't argue. You agreed. And because you did (and few people ever do), the agent feels comfortable with you and totally unthreatened. And they are also much more open to your tactfully communicated solution.

Now that we've seen where agreement accomplishes the first part, the next is to help him live in the solution.

For instance, you might say: "I know one reason for this very important rule is to make sure the rooms are clean and ready for your guests. That makes a lot of sense, and is one reason I always enjoy staying here. I'm wondering, *just if it's not too much trouble,* would it be possible for you to check to see if there is a room ready that I could check in to?"

Then, as he's checking, simply say, "If you can't do it, I'll definitely understand." (This is what I call an out phrase and it's very powerful. We'll see why in chapter 53.)

I can tell you from personal experience and the vast number of emails I receive that this works. Every time? Not necessarily. But, indeed, if there is a room that is ready, you will most likely be able to check in and get one of the really good ones.

Had you reacted to the desk clerk's initial statement, chances are he or she would have become defensive and an argument would have ensued. Instead, you responded, communicated understanding, and provided a solution that he was only too happy to agree with.

Remember, first agree. Then (and *only* then) persuade.

EGO REPAIR

I t was 9:45 p.m. at customs at the Toronto International Airport, and things were progressing nicely. I was about to be checked through by the last person, my ride was waiting to take me to the hotel, and I'd be set for a good night's sleep and ready to present the following morning. But there would be a snag.

As usual, everyone at Immigration had been exceedingly polite (I've found that Canadians, on the whole, tend to be extremely gracious people). Walking toward the officer at the final clearance checkpoint I smiled at her, and received a smile in return.

With the upcoming transaction positively framed, what came next was unexpected.

When she asked why I was coming into Canada, I told her I was there to speak at a national convention of financial advisers. That's when her entire demeanor suddenly changed. "You are a seminar leader then?" she asked. When I answered in the affirmative, she seemed to become rather agitated.

"Exactly what are you speaking on?" As you can probably tell, she did not ask with benign curiosity but with more than a bit of negative expectation.

When I told her my topic, she asked me to clarify. When I did so, she said she didn't understand and asked me to clarify further. When I complied, she began asking questions about my client company, its history, the number of people who would be attending my presentation, and other matters I knew were not relevant to the situation (I've spoken in Canada enough times to have a working understanding of what they need to know in order to comply with immigration laws).

Obviously, something was wrong. Why the sudden change?

There are often two reasons for the type of negativity or antagonism this person was displaying—the reason they give you and the real reason. Often, they themselves are not consciously aware of the difference in those reasons, though this was not one of those occasions.

Something was bothering the immigration officer that was not yet apparent to me, but I'd need to figure it out soon or I'd be spending hours at the immigration office.

She asked if I would specifically define myself as a "seminar leader, consultant, lecturer, or speaker." Actually, I'd define myself as a really nice guy but I was fairly sure that wasn't the correct answer. I was pretty certain at this point that anything I said could and would be held against me.

When I told her I could most accurately be defined as a speaker, she made a *tsk-tsk-tsk* sound.

Important aside: in a situation like this, regardless of whether you feel angry, confused, bewildered, abused, et cetera, do your best to keep your wits about you. Control your emotions. Maintain a sincere, warm smile and display extreme patience and politeness in your responses. A person acts rudely because she "wants" you to become flustered and lose control. You have somehow (most likely unintentionally) pushed her buttons and now she wants to push yours. Do not raise your voice or insult her. Keep cool!

Her next question dealt with whether I was receiving an honorarium or a fee for my engagement—honorarium denoting little money, and fee implying lots of money. Now, despite the fact that I guessed she'd be much happier if I said honorarium, I told her the truth and said I was receiving a fee.

Another very important point: aside from the fact that lying is generally wrong (unless you or your loved ones are in danger), it also will often backfire. For instance, had I said honorarium and she detained me in order to check, and found out the size of the fee I was receiving, I could truly have been in hot water and possibly even sent back home without further discussion. My client would not have been happy. No, the truth is usually best.

IMMIGRATION OFFICER: "Mr. Burg, let me tell you the problem."

She proceeded to cite a rule that should not have been an issue. While I knew her reason was simply a rationalization, I listened with respect and attentiveness and did not interrupt.

ME: "Well, I completely understand what you're saying. You have rules that must be followed. I'm a guest in your country and I respect that fact entirely and will do my best to comply."

Yes, I agreed with her. Remember the principle of agreement from the last chapter: nobody argues with himself!

Now, even though she still had not quite leveled with me regarding the actual problem, it had to come out soon. And it did.

IMMIGRATION OFFICER: "Do you know [name of a successful American speaker/author]?"

ME: "I know of him."

IMMIGRATION OFFICER: "He came through here several months ago, and he was the most obnoxious, arrogant person who has ever . . ."

Ahh, there we have it. That was her problem and, of course, now my problem. She had been insulted and hurt by someone who, on the surface, was similar to me. Now she was—I believe, unconsciously— taking it out on me and making me pay for it. After all, I was right there in front of her. This is what the whole incident had been about. It had nothing to do with anything other than that.

Two huge Ultimate Influence Principles apply here.

1. People make major decisions based on limited information (i.e., their belief system). I'm an author/speaker from the United States, hence, I must be exactly like the rude American speaker she'd previously encountered.

2. The ego rules. Her feelings had been hurt. If someone's ego is bruised, she will act in a way not in accordance with her natural persona. Remember, when first meeting her she seemed very nice, and I got the feeling she probably really is.

Now it would be easy to move her to my side. She had been able to get all of those bad feelings out her system and to let me know she had the power to control my situation. That was fine with me. Of course, it wouldn't be right for me to agree with her and insult the other speaker. Instead, I simply said, "I just appreciate your patience and helping me proceed through this."

Yes, I thanked her *in advance* for what I wanted her to do. Said correctly, this will persuade the person to do exactly what you thanked her for.

IMMIGRATION OFFICER: "Well, I guess I shouldn't be talking like that but he was really difficult. You're obviously not like that. Anyway, Mr. Burg, I appreciate your patience and how honest you've been with me. Have a great stay in Toronto."

People are ruled—they are *driven*—by their feelings, emotions, and egos. Mary Kay Ash said, "Everyone wears an invisible sign around their neck that says, 'Make me feel important.'" So, to solve this difficult challenge with the immigration agent, my goal had to be to reinstate her feeling of importance.

Hey, glad I could be of help.

THE POWER OF HANDWRITTEN NOTES

I f you've ever attended one of my live presentations or read any of my books, you know how much I value handwritten, personalized notes, especially after meeting someone for the first time, doing business with them, receiving a referral, et cetera.

That's not to say emails aren't great; I certainly send a lot of them. However, there's a time and place for everything. And in many situations, practically nothing makes an impact like a handwritten note of appreciation. Talk about making someone feel good about themselves! The fact that you obviously took time out of your day and made the effort to do this communicates to them that they are important and special.

Even *before* the birth of email and social media, which makes it so easy to quickly type a few words and send them directly to someone, relatively few people constantly and consistently wrote thank-you notes. Those who did stood out far from the crowd. Now with the prevalence of technology, even fewer people write them, and those who do are positioned much more powerfully than the vast majority who don't.

I suggest you use a specially designed note card, 8½ by 3 inches (so it fits in a standard envelope) of seventy- to eighty-pound card stock.* Remember, it is not a postcard but a note card. Put it in the envelope, use a regular or commemorative stamp (not a metered stamp), and handwrite the person's name and address on the envelope. Also, use blue rather than black ink. It's a bit less formal and more personal.

Influencers write handwritten notes, and lots of them. They find reasons to write them and they send them to all sorts of people. In addition to prospects, customers, and clients, send a note to your waiter, mechanic, or any service person who takes good care of you. Send one to the police officer who was responsive to your call or the nurse at the hospital who took extra good care of your child.

While sending a handwritten note directly to the person who helped you will make their day, if you want to take an extra step that's even more powerful, send a letter to his or her boss. This should usually be typed rather than handwritten.

Not only is sending a handwritten note a nice thing to do for everyone involved but the next time you come across them, do business with them, or need their help, you will be at the top of their emotional list.

Of course, it goes without saying that if you are applying for a job, you should always send a handwritten thank-you note to the person who interviewed you.

And if you're a parent, I urge you to teach your children the importance of handwritten notes. Make sure they know that these notes of thanks, whether to their teachers, professors, or the person to whom they applied for a job, might be the difference-maker in helping them achieve their goal.

---

* If you want to see my preferred setup, go to www.burg.com/notecard.

27

EDIFICATION—A POWERFUL
KEY TO INFLUENCE

To edify, according to one dictionary definition, is to build. When you edify people, you build them up in the minds of other people and, perhaps most important, in their own minds, as well.

Edify people, to others and to themselves, even for the things you *wish* they would do. They'll soon begin to believe their own press and start adopting the traits and behaviors for which they are being praised.

When edifying people to one another (a practice I often refer to as Reverse Gossip), you'll create goodwill between them. And these good feelings will come back to you as the creator of this community of benevolence.

A few examples include:

> "Jim sure is precise in the way he fills out his reports."
> "Mary, I love how you always handle people with such great tact."
> "Mr. and Mrs. Jones, our service representative Steve is fantastic. He'll take great care of you and make sure you're comfortable every step of the way. Steve, Tom and Mary

Jones just took ownership of our latest widget and I appreciate you taking such terrific care of them."

"My spouse is the most supportive partner in the world."

"I'm always amazed by how Kathy can organize a team."

When in doubt as to what to say *about* someone or *to* someone—*edify!* You can hardly ever go wrong.

Find a way to genuinely edify others and your influence will accelerate quickly. It's that powerful!

28

DO YOU LOOK FOR DISAGREEMENT?

Some people simply cannot resist the opportunity to disagree. And these days they have an ideal platform for their contrarian opinions on various social media like Facebook, Twitter, LinkedIn, and blog comment sections.

It usually goes something like this. Someone posts a principle-based statement that clearly holds true in context: "Unnecessary fears can stop you from taking that important step toward success. Take action despite your fear!"

Then someone else posts a response pointing to the one exception: "But what about those times when you would be putting your life in danger?"

A heated back-and-forth begins when the original poster responds in annoyance: "You are a moron. Did I not begin with the words, 'UNNECESSARY fear'? Get a life!"

The responder rarely agrees but perhaps feels good about eliciting a reaction in that oh-so-strange way argumentative people do.

This kind of an exchange is prevalent online but also happens off-line in one-on-one, group, and presenter/audience conversations.

Please don't misunderstand my point. There's certainly nothing wrong with questioning a statement. In fact, how cool is it when, regardless of the medium, we can all learn from one another through honest and respectful dialogue?

But few appreciate the person who just has to point out the one contrarian example in an otherwise sound and principle-based statement. Doing this comes across not only as argumentative but as ego-based, as well. While it might gain the outspoken critic attention, it will not gain them influence.

Again, there is nothing wrong with respectfully disagreeing. If you're going to do so, and in a way that is most persuasive, keep the following suggestions in mind:

1. **Think about it first.** Respond rather than react. Taking a moment before pulling the trigger and hitting send (or voicing your opinion in person) will rarely come back to haunt you. But it might save you from an unnecessary or counterproductive action.

2. **Look first for where you agree.** Only then—if you feel it necessary—note the flaw. While many general principles have exceptions within certain contexts, it's not usually necessary to point them out. First, ask yourself if doing so will add value to the conversation. If not, don't comment.

3. **Use tact.** If you feel it must be communicated publicly (and at times it should be), do so politely, tactfully, and respectfully. For example, say, "I appreciate your thought. Just wondering, what . . ." or, "If I may ask . . ." When possible, do this privately so that you don't appear to be calling them out or trying to embarrass them.

4. **Do a final check.** Before hitting send or asking the question, ask yourself: am I motivated by a genuine desire to add value or am I disagreeing simply as a way to get attention, begin an argument, or feel better about myself? This is the ultimate question in order

to determine whether your comment is ego based, and if so, whether you are in control of your ego or your ego is in control of you.

If massaging your ego is the basis for looking for and voicing your disagreement, then realize that you will offend the ego of the person with whom you are disagreeing. Is that likely to cause them to embrace your thoughts and be persuaded by you? No, it will have the exact opposite effect. And that serves no one.

Whether online or offline, there is a better way to agree and disagree, and a way to make yourself heard. Do you want to be taken seriously by others and expand your influence? Then make sure when you do this, it's for the right reason.

Now, feel free to disagree with me.

29

COMPLIMENT THE UNCOMPLIMENTED

I t's often said that a person who is nice to their superiors but not to the waiter is not a nice person. After all, how a person treats those who are not in a position to help them says a lot about his or her character.

Yet, complimenting—or even simply being polite to—a person who is not usually complimented, shown respect, or even acknowledged by others can also have a tremendous impact on how far that person will go out of their way to help you, should the need arise. While this is not the *reason* to be nice to them, it is often the result.

What a nice way to live life when you consistently go out of your way to compliment those who serve others but are not usually treated with a great deal of respect. From the street sweeper to the skycap, from the hotel doorman to, well, any service person, aside from tipping or a quick thank-you, do you refer to them as sir or ma'am? Do you acknowledge them with kindness? Do you genuinely think of them as important and significant, and does it show?

Yes, it makes a definite difference to their self-esteem. It also reflects how far they'll go out of their way to make sure you are happy. And you never know when that will come in handy.

Of course, that isn't *why* you do it. You do it because it's the right way to be, the right thing to do, and because it aligns with your value system in terms of treating others. However, don't argue with the results. Being the type of person who compliments and genuinely respects others will also pay off in big dividends.

It might also pay off indirectly, as well. Those who might be deciding whether you'd be good to do business with, or even become more involved with socially, are watching how you treat others. For instance, there are companies where managers observe job applicants in the reception area before bringing them in for the formal interview. When people don't think they're being watched, they will behave like they usually do. This gives employers an opportunity to see how would-be employees interact with those they don't necessarily need to be nice to—the receptionist, other people in the waiting area, and so forth.

That being said, being nice to someone—complimenting the uncomplimented—might do nothing more than ensure that the other person feels a little better about themselves. And isn't that reason enough?

CAUGHT IN THE ACT! . . . OF DOING
SOMETHING RIGHT

Remember the classic *The One Minute Manager,* by Drs. Kenneth Blanchard and Spencer Johnson? One of their most famous pieces of advice for leaders and managers in effectively working with their team members was to, "Catch them in the act of doing something right."

That doesn't mean you bury your head in the sand and ignore those who are doing things wrong. Depending upon the situation—and as we discussed earlier—we often need to tactfully, and with empathy, provide correction. Yet, as Mark Sanborn points out in his book *Fred 2.0,* "It's ironic, isn't it, how poor performance tends to get more attention than good performance? We effectively feed our problems and starve our star performers." In other words, how often do we ignore the people doing things right . . . only because they're not doing anything wrong?

When you catch someone in the act of doing something right, make sure you acknowledge it verbally and, if appropriate, make sure everyone else—in the office, home, or wherever you are—sees and hears you do it.

When the store cashier handles the customer in front of you with patience and empathy, make sure you let him know you noticed and tell him how impressed you are. If there are others around, it wouldn't hurt to lavish your praise in a voice loud enough for them to hear as well.

And, of course, isn't it great to catch a child in the act of doing something right, and verbally reward him or her for that?

As the saying goes, whether positive or negative:

Behavior that gets rewarded gets repeated.

Ultimate Influencers excel in making people feel genuinely good about themselves by rewarding good behavior. And don't be afraid to encourage excellence by acknowledging it in advance. You are giving that person a worthy ideal to live up to.

"I APPRECIATE YA"

While we're talking about the influential power of compliments and gratitude, here's a final thought on acknowledgments.

After completing a quick purchase or some other business transaction with someone, instead of just saying thank you, let them know you appreciate them.

A genuine smile and a quick "I appreciate you" or "I appreciate ya" work just fine.

It's that little *extra* special touch that separates you from everyone else—even the polite people who say thank you—and makes you memorable in someone else's mind.

You become that person they'll go out of their way to please during the next transaction. Do this just a couple of times and note the surprised and delighted expressions on their faces. It becomes habit-forming.

Thank you for taking the time to read this . . . I appreciate ya!

SECTION FIVE

Set the Proper Frame

Do This Correctly and You Are 80 Percent of the Way to the Win/Win Outcome You Desire

> The peak efficiency of knowledge and strategy is to make conflict altogether unnecessary.
>
> —Thomas Cleary, from the Translator's Introduction to the classic *The Art of War,* by Sun Tzu

A two-year-old falls down unexpectedly. He isn't hurt but instinctually knows he wasn't supposed to fall. He looks at Mom and Dad for an interpretation of what happened. If they laugh as though it's funny, he'll probably laugh. If they panic and act upset, he will most likely begin to cry. In either case, Mom and Dad *unintentionally* set the frame that led to the outcome.

Actually, adults are very much the same. Notice this the next time you cross paths with a stranger. If you smile (a *friendly* frame), they'll usually smile. If you say hello, they'll usually say hello. The opposite is also true. Usually, we can influence another's response by controlling the stimulus, *our* action.

This is also known as setting the frame.

Recall the story I told at the beginning of section two about nearly hitting a man in the parking lot. While it reinforced the power and benefit of controlling my own emotions, the very positive outcome had a lot to do with *resetting* another's frame. While the man leaving his car was in an anger frame, I immediately went into friendly apology frame. Just by doing this one thing, his attitude did a complete 180. I guarantee that had I bought into his original frame and stayed there, the situation would've gotten ugly.

Nine times out of ten, the other person will follow your frame. Always remember:

> In any interpersonal transaction or situation, a frame will be set. The only question is, Who will set it—you or the other person? Make sure it is you.

Since the other person is most likely not even aware of this concept, the chances of a positive transaction are greatly enhanced if you are the one who sets the frame.

You have the power to set positive frames from which others—in all situations, both business and personal—can feel good about themselves and feel good about you. If this is not part of your usual style, it takes a bit of work to get used to doing it. Because of that, most people won't do it. Those who do, have a *decided* advantage as they make their way through life. It is so worth it!

Reach out with a pleasant countenance, a genuine smile on your face, and a friendly hello. Assume this person, if given the chance, would like to respond positively to that kind of attitude. Chances are they would, and they will. It's up to you though. The master of people skills and ultimate influence doesn't wait for the other person to set the frame. Instead, they take the initiative and make sure the most productive frame is set.

But what if they have already set the frame? What if they have entered this transaction deciding (unconsciously, as it practically always is) that they are not going to play nice?

Good news! Just as in our earlier parking lot example, you can reset their frame simply by setting your own.

The quote by Thomas Cleary at the beginning of this section was an interpretation of and a tie-in to a particular lesson by Sun Tzu that, in terms of war, "To overcome others' armies without fighting is the best of skills."

We can paraphrase the above statement and apply it to Ultimate Influence and conflict resolution by saying that . . .

To influence without conflict is the best of skills.

In other words, the best way to go from adversary to ally is to ensure they never become an adversary in the first place.

And that's why properly setting the frame is so very important. Of course, if their frame is already set (as was the case with the person I almost clipped in the parking lot), the next best thing is to reset their frame.

Setting the frame, resetting the frame . . . controlling the frame. This is exactly what we will focus on in this section.

And once you accomplish this, you will be 80 percent of the way toward obtaining the win/win result you desire.

32

POSITIVE EXPECTATION WORKS, BUT NOT WHY YOU *THINK* IT DOES

You're about to go into a sales presentation with a prospect you've heard can be a real bear. Or you're about to ask the customer service representative with a sour look on her face if you can exchange an item without the receipt. Perhaps you need to ask one of your vendors to rush an order knowing he always seems put out when asked to do that.

We face a number of situations every day that would sure go a lot more smoothly if the other person would be kind, smiling, and ready to help.

Both for long-term and immediate results, when you want to bring out a response in a person that meets your needs, act toward that person in the way you'd like them to respond. Yes, approach them believing they're going to want to give you what you desire.

Before you think I'm totally crazy, talking hocus-pocus or suggesting that just by thinking about something you'd like to happen it will, please know that's not the case.

Expecting someone to be helpful doesn't change them, it changes you. And that is what changes them.

What *will* happen is that by predetermining someone's attitude or action in your own mind as being positive and helpful, *you take on a corresponding attitude*. Yes, *you* change, which transfers directly into him or her changing their original attitude and acting in the appropriate solution-oriented manner.

Why? Because if you display gratitude and appreciation for their kindness, they are going to respond by living up to those very feelings you have about them.

When you communicate how much you like and respect them for their ability to find a solution, they are going to be motivated to live up to your obviously very correct appraisal of them.

It Works Both Ways

Let's look at two opposite approaches to a situation and the likely results.

You've been directed to see a particular official at your local city hall. You know he has the reputation for being difficult, leaning on his rule book to justify his unhelpfulness. You expect a fight, so you go in with your guard up. And while you manage to somewhat hide your scowl of disgust, you do wear a serious expression so he knows you mean business.

But what if you walked up to him with a genuine smile on your face, greeted him with a polite hello, and absolutely expected (and communicated the energy of) a positive and helpful response?

Which attitude is more likely to turn this potential enemy into a friend, this possible adversary into an ally? Which frame do you feel would be best to set if your goal was to influence and persuade this person?

Yes, this works, in amazing ways with practically everyone, and practically every single time.

Before dismissing this, do it with sincerity several times. I guarantee you'll walk away in amazement and it will change the way you approach the normally difficult people you must deal with. More important, it will change the results you usually get, and you'll find that this makes your actions much more productive and your life a lot less stressful!

This happens to be one of the most powerful methods of influence and persuasion there is. Practice until it becomes habit.

Setting a positive expectation is a habit that will pay off for you throughout your life. It will also be a source of continual amazement to you and those who see you do it.

A Smile: The Ultimate Frame-Setter

You may have noticed the importance of a smile when utilizing the above method for creating a helpful attitude in another person. While a smile may not be everything, there is perhaps nothing more powerful in beginning a relationship, conversation, or in overcoming an interpersonal challenge. A warm, genuine, sincere smile that emanates from your heart, from the inside out.

Smile at another before the transaction and you've set a magnificently benevolent frame from the get-go.

The majority of both personal and business relationship challenges could most likely be resolved peacefully with a smile, followed by genuine concern for the other's needs. The fact that most people *don't* do this will only make it easier for you to find yourself ahead in the game.

When you must speak with someone's supervisor about a particular challenge, your smile will bring down his or her walls of resistance, and set the tone (the frame) for a pleasant win/win discussion and positive result.

One main reason is that you've just separated yourself from practically everyone else whose greeting to her is a defensive, angry, or intimidating look.

In *Working with Emotional Intelligence*, Daniel Goleman writes, "It happens that smiles are the most contagious emotional signal of all, having an almost irresistible power to make other people smile in return."

That's powerful!

And very true! Read any good book on people skills and there will be at least a mention of the power of a smile. Dale Carnegie devoted an entire segment of his classic *How to Win Friends and Influence People* to the powerful influence of a sincere smile.

How Do You Get to (Dale) Carnegie Hall? Practice!

Fortunately, it's very easy to learn how to smile effectively. If necessary, simply imagine something that truly brings you joy and think of that before you need to smile. After a few practice sessions, you'll be able to bring forth that smile naturally.

It seems very few people smile without a particular reason. But that doesn't have to include you. Get that smile on your face before you deal with anyone; the service person, government bureaucrat, your boss, the waitperson, your spouse and children—everyone. Get yourself ready for that person to like you and smile back at you! Remember:

A smile is the ultimate frame-setter.

You can employ this simple action every day with amazing results. You'll be delighted (sometimes astounded!) by the special, over-the-top assistance you'll so often receive . . . just because the person is so positively affected by your smile.

33

FRAMING YOUR INFLUENCE IN YOUR FIRST CONVERSATION

Yes, your influence with someone begins the very instant you meet them. Intuitively, then, it might seem that whether they are a potential sales prospect or referral source, someone within your company or a person within your social circle, you need to come on strong. In other words, establish your high level of influence with a powerful defining statement about yourself and your business.

Um, no. Actually, the way to effectively frame your influence is to do just the opposite.

Focus on them. Invest 99.9 percent of the conversation in asking them questions about themselves and their business, their family, their interests.

When you make them feel good about themselves (and there is rarely a more effective way than by being *genuinely* interested in them), they are more likely to want to get to know you; they will like you, and begin to trust you.

Have you ever been in a conversation with someone who let you do practically all the talking? Didn't you leave the conversation thinking to yourself, *What a fascinating conversationalist that person is!*? You also probably felt really good about them, as well.

You can do the same by asking questions. But not just any questions. Ask questions that specifically make this person feel good about himself or herself. I call these Feel-Good Questions. The following are just a couple of them.* Ask just these first two and you'll be amazed at how quickly you can develop a positive rapport.

1. **How did you get started in the _____ business?** Other than celebrities, how often are people asked to share their story? When you ask, you've immediately set yourself apart from most others.

2. **What do you enjoy most about what you do?** This is another rarely asked question, and of course the question itself elicits a positive response.

The One Key Question

Imagine how good this person will feel when you ask:

> "How can I know if someone I'm speaking with would be a good prospect for you?"

Talk about immediately communicating value to another person's life!

Of course, if what they do isn't sales related, simply replace the word prospect with contact, connection, or something similar. Or ask how to know if someone you're speaking with is someone they'd like to meet. The principle remains the same.

Other questions you can ask are about their family, their recreation, or about other topics you discover are of interest to *them*. Are they involved in a cause? How much do you think they'd like to be asked about that?

---

* For my full list of my Feel-Good Questions, visit www.burg.com/10Q.

I remember speaking with the CEO of a company and discovering his daughter had just graduated college. After asking what line of work she was looking to explore, I asked how I could best identify a good connection for her. The dad was pleased by the question and let me know how I could help. My mind was already going through my mental contact database and I was able to introduce him to someone who gave his daughter an internship.

It worked out well for everyone involved, including me. No, I didn't have any attachment to the results. But results happen due to the gravitational pull of your influence, and influence happens through focusing on the needs, wants, and desires of others!

SOMETIMES, IT'S GOOD TO *LET*'EM SEE YOU SWEAT

On the first day of fourth grade, Miss Kadlik, a beautiful, elegant "older woman" (after all, she was twenty-three) stood in front of us to introduce herself. Her smile was reassuringly sweet, as was her personality and entire essence.

The first words she uttered taught me a lesson that I have never forgotten.

She said, "I just want all of you to know that I'm just out of college, this is my very first class, and I'm very, very nervous right now."

You could have heard the proverbial pin drop. We were silent.

What? We must all have been thinking: *a teacher . . . nervous? What could she possibly be nervous about?*

Here was her intuitive brilliance, which you can utilize in dealing with stressful and intimidating situations.

She admitted her fear. She trusted us with those feelings. She made us her partners in what was, for her, a very stressful situation.

And we responded to it. She immediately won us over, and although we still couldn't believe a teacher was nervous because of us, we were determined to make sure she would overcome her challenges.

So often, whether in business or interpersonal situations, we are afraid to admit our fears, to let our guard down, concerned that the dogs and lions will surround us if we do.

I'm sure you know the antiperspirant catchphrase, "Never let 'em see you sweat." In other words, if others know you're not totally calm, cool, collected, and in control, they might respect you less, step all over you, and otherwise take advantage of you.

Typically, I've found that not to be true. Ninety-nine times out of a hundred, if you'll let people know you are not all that, and even that you have your fears and trepidations, they will do their best to put you at ease, will unconsciously root for you to win, and will often even become your partner in doing so. Of course, all situations are different so, while understanding the meaning, judge each situation accordingly. Sometimes, not letting them see you sweat is *exactly* the correct advice!

People generally relate to those who seem human and experience occasional lapses of self-confidence, as do they. While the slick person may overwhelm and dazzle, they typically are not as relatable as the "real" person.

In his excellent book *Give and Take*, award-winning Wharton professor and researcher Dr. Adam Grant calls this "powerless communication." In other words, by coming from a more humble position, one of vulnerability and honesty, you are actually much more likely to gain the trust and acceptance of others.*

It seems to me that this powerless communication is actually the ultimate power-*full* communication.

So while being confident, prepared, and excellent at what you do is a winning course to take, during those times when, for whatever reason, you feel overwhelmed, under-confident, and just a little scared, admit it, and win.

Maybe even let 'em see you sweat.

---

* As professor Grant adds, "Expressing vulnerability is only effective if the audience receives other signals establishing the speaker's competence." This was certainly the case with Miss Kadlik.

35

THE RANSBURGER PIVOT

When involved in an intellectual debate with someone you'd like to persuade, always begin with a point on which you both agree. This way, the person will see that you're not just looking to argue in order to be disagreeable.

Even more important, he'll understand that you both really want the same result; you just have different views on how to get there. That's much more acceptable, and engenders cooperation rather than conflict.

From that point of engagement, you can now *pivot* into making your point. Since the new point you are about to make is based on a current point with which you now both agree, it will be easier for the other person to accept this new conclusion. This is called the Ransberger Pivot, developed by Ray Ransberger and Marshall Fritz.

Because politics can be one of the most potentially explosive situations, let's use a very highly charged issue as an example.

Let's say you believe that adults should be free to make their own retirement investment choices. Your friend, however, believes that the government should be in charge of this and that it can do it more effectively via the current Social Security system. He states that he believes that "People like you are heartless" for not taking into consideration the fact that too many people will not take care to provide for themselves.

He has already set a frame of conflict by insulting you rather than simply addressing the actual issue. Ego offended, you might, with a louder-than-usual voice, say, "The current Social Security system is nothing more than a pay-as-you-go Ponzi scheme that's forcibly bilked the American public out of its own retirement money, greatly hurts the poor, and is functionally bankrupt, not to mention totally unconstitutional."

How likely is it that the other person will suddenly be accepting of your view? Not very likely. All you're doing is arguing. You're telling him he's wrong, and he's not interested in that. Remember, facts don't persuade—*people* persuade.

Let's try another way. This time, in a calm, respectful voice, you begin with a premise with which you're certain the two of you are in total agreement. You say: "John, I appreciate your thoughts and, like you, I want our country to be one in which not one person has to suffer in their old age for lack of money, or in any way be a burden to their family or society."

Ahhh, since that's exactly what John wants as well, he may now be more open to learning how you think this can be accomplished. Rather than being angry, he might simply ask you a question, such as, "Well, okay, but how would you ensure that those who've paid into the system all these years don't lose the money that's rightfully theirs?"

Only *After* the New Frame Has Been Set Will the Facts Be Heard

Now, assuming you have the facts in front of you, you can calmly, kindly, and respectfully educate him. And he may or may not agree with you, which is his right. But you would *never* have even gotten to the point where he's willing to listen had you not first taken the time to show him where you agreed with his basic premise and that you actually have the same goal.

So you begin by saying, "Like you, I want . . ." fill in the blank. Then you pivot in the direction you choose to go. This surprises him because he expects you to go right from the last point he made and launch into an argument. But you do just the opposite. The result is that he becomes less defensive and perhaps more open to an alternative view.

As you saw, I added the lead-in phrase, "I appreciate your thoughts." This provides a buffer and sets up the pivot even more effectively. Or words like, "I agree with . . . ," "I'm in complete agreement with your . . . ," or "I appreciate your feelings about this" are all excellent lead-ins.

The Ransburger Pivot will work in practically every situation, not just politics. First, show where you both share the same basic premise and ultimate desire or goal. Then, with tact and respect, communicate the facts of the issue.

Master this and your Influence Quotient (IQ) will go sky high.

36

THE VALUE OF
THE CORRECT PHRASE

was at my local Dunkin' Donuts for my usual Sunday treat of two donuts, two cups of coffee, and three hours of reading (in between saying hello to some regulars).

This was a new store that had had their official grand opening just the day before, complete with celebrity guests and free merchandise, one being a Dunkin' travel cup.

Having a bunch left over, the employees decided to give them away to those standing in line. The assistant manager, a very nice young lady, handed them out while saying, "We had these left over from yesterday so we're giving them away."

While the gesture was nice, it was not nearly as effective in building goodwill as it could have been.

Why not? The words she used communicated no value to the customer, only to the store. She might as well have said, "We wanted to get rid of 'em yesterday but since we didn't, we're going to pawn them off on you right now."

Instead, she could have communicated value and planted the seeds of positive goodwill simply by saying, "These are for you as our way of saying thank you for being our valued customer. They're guaranteed to keep your coffee hot, and in the cup instead of your lap." Add a warm smile and it would have gone over great!

Of course, the cup itself has the same *actual* value regardless of the language she used. But its *perceived* value would either rise or fall based on how she communicated that value to her customers.

Always, always, always remember this:

It's not about you. It's about them.

Keep those seven words in mind whenever you are attempting to express value to another person, whether in a personal or business context. People don't care how it affects you. They care how it affects *them*. This is something that great influencers and persuaders always understand, keep in mind, and communicate!

37

"WHAT CAN I DO TO HELP?"

"What can I do to help?" This question is the one often asked by professional educator Joni Altshuler when she walks into a meeting with a parent she has been warned is irate.

Ms. Altshuler works in a very challenging school situation. In her role, she is often in the position of dealing with parents who may or may not have a legitimate reason to be angry.

As such, it's very important for her to set the proper frame. Or, in many of these cases, reset a negative frame already embraced by the parents.

According to Altshuler, "Most of the parents expect to meet someone who is primed to defend themselves. The reason they expect this is because that is what they have always experienced."

Her point is so profound. Sad as that is, it also tells you how very simple it is to separate yourself from practically everyone else.

"Instead," continues Ms. Altshuler, "in a friendly, compassionate, but calm way, I simply ask, 'What can I do to help?' In other words, how can we all work together to make this situation right for everyone, most importantly, their child?"

Now *that's* a great reframe!

Her method is very similar to a well-known negotiation tactic in which, when dealing with a difficult person, the negotiator might ask, "Mr. Thomas, what is it you'd like to have result from our discussion?"

The coolness and calmness of the negotiator diffuses the other person, communicates that they (the negotiator) won't be rattled by a person acting nasty and/or emotionally, and indicates that mutual satisfaction is their goal and can in fact be attained.

Hostage negotiators will also use this tactic. They'll come right out, whether by bullhorn or telephone, and ask the hostage taker, "What is it you'd like to have happen?" or "What is it you want to accomplish through this?"

When in the act of influencing another, control your own emotions, present a calm, self-controlled front, and set or reset the frame by simply asking the other person, "What can I do to help?"

They will be happy to give you the answer, and the conversation will take a much more mutually beneficial turn.

WIN BY MAKING
THE OTHER'S CASE FIRST

t's well documented that the sixteenth U.S. president, Abraham Lincoln, was a true master at turning enemies into friends and adversaries into allies.

Before Mr. Lincoln was president, he was a very successful lawyer. While he was known to be extremely well prepared for his cases and very competent at presenting the facts, he also did something that established a positive frame for him and his clients that gave him a decided advantage.

Mr. Lincoln would typically begin his opening arguments by summing up the *other side's* case. He would point out the positive aspects of their position, and how very worthy they were of consideration. In fact, it was said that if you walked into the courtroom at that time, you'd actually think he was representing that side of the case.

By doing this, Mr. Lincoln was establishing his credibility with the judge and jury, and demonstrating that both sides had a legitimate view and that he was seeking only the truth. Wow! Now, when it was time to present his client's side, he really poured it on, providing fact after fact, point after point in order to make his client's case.

But he could get away with doing that because his credibility was now so high.

After all, the judge and jury reasoned that if he was so willing to give credibility to the viewpoint of the other side, he *must* be honest and speaking straight from his heart.

You Can Utilize This, Too!

One of the most effective ways to positively and gently disarm a person with whom you are having a disagreement, plus win them over to your side of the issue, is to first point out *their* side of the story.

Discover and vocalize the areas in which you agree with them—that is, show them you not only understand how they feel but that their view actually makes sense. When doing this, you in essence say to them, "Hey, there are two legitimate viewpoints here. You also have a reasonable argument—you have a view that is very worthy of consideration."

Now he or she can relax and let go of their defensiveness. They know they are not in a battle with someone who is out to get them, prove them wrong, or win at all costs.

He or she will have a newfound respect for you, and a newly opened mind toward the ideas you present. In fact, after doing this, the other person will typically point out the positive aspect of *your* side. And why not? You are now showing mutual respect, and working from a foundation of truth, kindness, and genuine interest in each other.

Whether you're presenting to a committee choosing between you and a competitor, or working out an issue with your spouse or friend, follow President Lincoln's lead.

Important Caveat

Understand that if you have a history with this person where win/ lose arguments and debate is the norm, it may take a couple of conversations before they'll be ready to accept your new attitude. Don't allow this to discourage you.

Very quickly they'll begin to see that you are simply searching for the truth—not just trying to be right at all costs.

In a sense, the key point in all this is humility, which leads to effective communication. When we are truly desirous of the truth and not just in winning an argument, people understand our intent and are much quicker to accept our position.

So when you establish the proper frame—respect for the other person's viewpoint—and proceed with kindness and tact, you will find yourself continually winning your cases.

HELP THEM
TO LIVE IN THE SOLUTION

One of my blog readers asked: "Being nice is great, but what if the person you're dealing with just isn't providing the help you need and you have no other option? Do you walk away and let it go at that? Why should their problem be your problem? That seems very dissatisfying to me. Do I have to simply accept that?"

That's an excellent question. Although there are times we do have to just walk away, those times are extremely rare. What we often need to do, however, is help the other person live in the solution instead of the problem. As long as this is accomplished with tact and kindness, everyone wins.

International leadership authority and best-selling author Dr. John Maxwell tells the story of the time he ordered a double cheeseburger. The counter person told him they don't serve double cheeseburgers. Dr. Maxwell asked, "Are you sure?" The young fellow replied, "Absolutely sure."

Dr. Maxwell, in a very polite manner, then asked, "I'll tell you what then—could you possibly make me two cheeseburgers, but on the second one, leave out the bread?"

The answer? "Sure, no problem."

No matter how solution-resistant the other person is, *your* goal is to always live in the solution. Indeed, *acknowledge* the problem. Pretending it's not there won't help. So acknowledge the problem but *focus* on the solution. As you do this more and more, it will become natural to you and half the fun of the persuasion process.

AVOID NEGATIVE FRAMING

Several years ago I was in a car driven by a friend of mine who had just moved down to Florida from Massachusetts. After stopping at a four-way stop sign, he did something he shouldn't have done. Immediately, a police car approached, flashing blues, sirens and all, and pulled us over.

The officer was very polite and professional and explained why he had pulled us over. My friend responded by saying, "That's not the law in Massachusetts."

Okay, here's a quiz. How do you think the officer responded?

A. "Oh, my fault then. I didn't realize you're from Massachusetts. Had I known that, I never would have had the audacity to stop you for doing something illegal here in FLORIDA."

B. "Well, everyone knows Massachusetts sets the standard for the way things are done everywhere else in the country, especially down here in Florida. Excuse me. Please,

AVOID NEGATIVE FRAMING | 143 |

go ahead and drive along, and I sincerely apologize for
bothering you."
C. "This isn't Massachusetts." Then he wrote up the ticket.

Of course, you guessed it. The answer is C. Amazingly enough, my
friend was flabbergasted. Now, you may know not to say something
like that to a police officer who is deciding whether or not to write
you a ticket. But it's interesting how often I hear someone begin a
conversation in a way that's almost guaranteed to upset the person
whom they, for whatever reason, want or need to win over.

We've seen how easy it is to create the environment for interpersonal success and Ultimate Influence. Then there is the very opposite.
These are words, phrases, and attitudes that will take a negative-
leaning situation and totally accelerate it into, at best, a difficult
situation, or at worst, an explosive one. In other words, they just
cause people to bristle.

The above was certainly one example. And so unnecessary with
just a bit of forethought.

Of course, even if we begin on the wrong foot by unnecessarily
upsetting the other person, we can still succeed; it'll just be a lot more
difficult. So why make dealing with a potential adversary any more
difficult than need be?

Instead, ask yourself what you can do at this very moment to set
the person at ease and make them as receptive as possible to you and
your message.

Think of some words and phrases you've used or heard in the past
that seem to upset or annoy people, and make a decision to erase
them from your vocabulary.

DON'T FALL VICTIM TO THE EITHER/OR

W ould you rather be wealthy or happy?"

"Are you a giver *or* a receiver?"

"Are you a nice person *or* do you finish first?"

Have you ever been presented with a question like one of the above where you are given an option of only two responses, even though more are available?

In our book *Go-Givers Sell More*, John David Mann and I referred to these as "treacherous dichotomies," also known as "false dilemmas." Either of the two can be defined as the unnecessary use of the word *or*.

In my opinion, the answers to all of the above questions should be . . . "YES!" Not one *or* the other.

Whether asked by someone without an agenda, or as a way of manipulating you into providing an answer based on contrived limitations, be careful that you don't allow others to place limits on your choices.

Most of us have—at one time or another—been asked by a salesperson, "Would you prefer to meet with me on Tuesday at ten, or Wednesday at two?" That's called the alternate of choice and, when utilized genuinely, is an effective way of *framing* a choice for the prospect, making it easier for them to grasp a convenient time.

On the other hand, as the prospect, you are allowed to politely say, "Actually, neither one would work for me." In other words, don't feel obligated to operate within another person's frame.

A person attempting to get you to buy into their philosophy, purchase their product, or say yes to something else that you wouldn't normally say yes to, might use this false dilemma in order to manipulate you into doing just that.

How do you avoid this trap? Whenever you are given a choice between only two things—one *or* the other—simply slow down and allow yourself to think before answering. Ask yourself if those are *really* the only two logical choices, if there is another choice that works better for you, or if you would prefer neither.

One important question to ask yourself might be, *Is there a reason this person would want me to think there are only these two choices?*

Just remember, the either/or, the treacherous dichotomy, the false dilemma, is nothing more than a frame. And you don't want somebody else setting your frame.

Of course, there are those occasions when there are only two legitimate choices, or one aspect of a thing *is* indeed more valid than the other. That's something you'll have to determine.

Life is a series of choices. Just be sure you are not *framed* into making a choice that does not serve you.

PERSUASION SECRETS
OF A TEN-YEAR-OLD

C hildren are intuitively persuasive. After all, unless their parents are extremely permissive, it's difficult for the typical child to get their way solely through forceful intimidation (i.e., kicking, screaming, whining) or through passive manipulation, such as being extra nice and/or cooperative but with an agenda.

While speaking at an event in Rock Hill, South Carolina, years ago, I heard a great story about a child that served as a wonderful example of Ultimate Influence.

Don and Hannah King's granddaughter, Christa, was then nine or ten years old. A year or so before the following conversation, Don and Hannah had promised to someday take her to Europe on one of their many overseas business trips. In early May, Hannah received a telephone call.

CHRISTA: "Grandma, when are you going to Europe?"

HANNAH: "In June."

CHRISTA: "Is this the year you are taking me with you, as you promised?"

HANNAH: "But, honey, it's only a month away and you don't even have a passport."

Well, that ended that conversation. Two weeks later, however, Hannah again answered her phone, only to hear the following:

CHRISTA: "Grandma, I've got it."

HANNAH: "You've got what?"

CHRISTA: "My passport. I'm ready to go to Europe with you and Grandpa."

HANNAH: "Well, you realize that Grandma and Grandpa will be in a lot of meetings, so sometimes you'll have to have a babysitter who doesn't even speak English."

CHRISTA: "I can handle it."

According to Hannah, Christa did great, and was a pleasure to take on the trip.

The principles of Christa's approach are well worth studying and repeating.

- First, ask in a way that assumes the answer you want.
- Second, give the person something admirable to live up to. When Hannah asked her grandma if this is "the year you are taking me with you, as you promised," what she was communicating was: Grandma, whom I love and respect so much, is this the year that you're going to show me that you are a person of your word who would never break a promise to her granddaughter whom she loves so much and for whom she wants to set an example of honesty and integrity?

➥ Third, if there is a problem, find the solution.
➥ Fourth, answer any objections.
➥ Fifth, live up to the promises you made, making persuasion
   with that party easier the next time around.

Well played, Christa. Well played!

CHANGE YOUR FRAME, CHANGE YOUR LIFE

n Vernon Howard's book *Esoteric Mind Power*, he writes: "If a mechanical robot made a rude remark to you, you would not feel offended, for your ego would not feel threatened by a mere machine. But because you fail to see that most people are equally mechanical, you attribute an ego to them, which causes your ego to think they can harm you. When you deeply see the man-machine behind human personality, you cannot be offended."

Now, whether you and I choose to see our fellow human beings as mere machines or not, what the author presented was a wonderful example of a personal reframe.

As we noted in chapter 33, a frame is the premise; the foundation from which everything else emanates. An outcome can occur only in relation to the context—or frame—in which it's set.

Throughout this section, we've focused mainly on setting the frame for others, or even resetting their already-existing negative frame into one that would be more productive for everyone involved.

Now let's do this for ourselves. The result will be a life of greater peace, empowerment, and effectiveness.

When we reframe, we make a decision to see an event differently than we usually might, if our normal interpretation would cause us to be unhappy. We choose a way of seeing and interpreting it that is now conducive to our happiness rather than to our misery. Yes, it's the same event, but since we are choosing to view it from a totally different frame, its effect on us is . . . well, totally different.

For example, take the event cited by Vernon Howard—someone makes a rude remark to you. Perhaps you usually see that as something to take personally. As a result, it can cause harm to your self-image and self-esteem, elicit a rude reply, try your patience, and generally ruin your day.

Instead, how could you take that event and *reframe* it so that it serves you and your happiness instead of undermining it? Understanding that, in the real world, different circumstances certainly call for different possible courses of action, here are a few ways to reframe a challenging encounter.

1. This is a terrific opportunity to practice my patience with people.
2. What an excellent opportunity to practice responding instead of reacting!
3. I am fortunate that I don't have the same problems and feeling of unhappiness that this poor guy obviously has.
4. What a tremendous opportunity to practice my influence skills and persuade this person to my point of view! (Only if appropriate, of course.)

From now on, focus on reframing every apparently negative situation—including both people and events—in a positive light. Practice by imagining various situations in advance and come up with a powerful reframe that you can utilize in the event it actually happens.

Picture challenging encounters with your boss, spouse, child, friend, and customer. Then imagine your car runs out of gas, you spill milk, slip on a banana peel (does anyone ever actually do that?), or anything else that would rankle you. What would be a positive reframe for you?

Again, this doesn't mean you're burying your head in the sand and ignoring the truth of a situation. What happened *did* happen. It simply means you are choosing to interpret it in a way that serves you rather than bothers you.

To the degree that you do this, you are also in a much better position to help others do the same. As a result, your ability to influence and persuade others grows and grows.

SECTION SIX

Communicate with Tact and Empathy

The Big Difference That Makes the Big Difference

Tact is the ability to tell a man he has an open mind when he has a hole in his head.

—A. Nonymous

Here's another lesson from an Ultimate Influence icon, Abraham Lincoln. This time in the form of a letter.

Major General Hooker:

General.

I have placed you at the head of the Army of the Potomac. Of course, I have done this upon what appears to me to be sufficient reasons. And yet I think it best for you to know that there are some things in regard to which, I am not quite satisfied with you. I believe you to be a brave and skillful soldier, which, of course, I like.

I also believe you do not mix politics with your profession, in which you are right. You have confidence in yourself, which is

valuable, if not an indispensable quality. You are ambitious,
which, within reasonable bounds, does good rather than harm.

But I think that during Gen. Burnside's command of the Army,
you have taken counsel of your ambition, and thwarted him as
much as you could, in which you did a great wrong to the country,
and to a most meritorious and honorable brother officer. I have
heard, in such a way as to believe it, of your recently saying that
both the Army and the Government needed a Dictator.

Of course it was not for this, but in spite of it, that I have given
you the command. Only those generals who gain successes, can set
up dictators. What I now ask of you is military success, and I will
risk the dictatorship. The government will support you to the
utmost of its ability, which is neither more nor less than it has
done and will do for all commanders. I much fear that the spirit
which you have aided to infuse into the Army, of criticizing their
Commander, and withholding confidence from him, will now turn
upon you. I shall assist you as far as I can, to put it down.

Neither you, nor Napoleon, if he were alive again, could get any
good out of an army, while such a spirit prevails in it. And now,
beware of rashness. Beware of rashness, but with energy, and
sleepless vigilance, go forward, and give us victories.

Yours very truly,
A. Lincoln

The above letter that President Lincoln wrote to Joseph Hooker
right after assigning the general to his new post is a terrific example
of tact. The president let Hooker know exactly where he fell short, but
without insulting him and damaging the relationship.

You can control your emotions, understand the clash of belief systems, acknowledge and deal successfully with another person's ego,
and set the proper frame and be further ahead in the influence and
persuasion process than 99.9 percent of the people on this planet.

But there's one more very important element that brings it all
home: tact and empathy.

I call these the Big Differentiators. In a sense, these qualities are like twins. One has to do with what you say and how you say it, while the other allows you to say it effectively.

As the above quote about the man with the hole in his head tells us, with tact you can make that point but allow the person to feel good about themselves, making them more open to embracing your message. With empathy, you can understand his feelings enough to know why you need to tell him this.

Tact and empathy. They are separate ideas but work hand in hand as the final principle to help you become a persuader and influencer of stratospheric proportion.

While we defined tact near the beginning of the book, I also went online to see what others had to say about it. The very first website I visited, wisdomcommons.org, provided what I felt was one of the most *brilliant* descriptions I've ever read:

> Tact is what allows us to honor both honesty and compassion in difficult conversations. It lets us speak truth in ways that other people are able to hear without becoming too threatened or hurt. To be tactful means choosing our timing as well as our words. Tact requires that we put ourselves in another person's place and think about their circumstances and feelings.

This description actually includes an excellent definition of empathy in the last sentence, highlighting why it is so important. Having and communicating empathy is what really makes you more likely to communicate with tact.

They work powerfully together. Unfortunately, most people are weak in both areas. There's absolutely no reason to remain that way.

While tact is mainly a skill it is also an attitude.

While empathy is mainly an attitude it is also a skill.

Fortunately, both can be learned and developed. And when you can count both of those among your personal strengths, you will have reached the level of a master of people skills, of persuasion, of Ultimate Influence.

And that's exactly what we'll focus on in this section.

CHAPTER

44

TACT—THE LANGUAGE OF STRENGTH

s there ever a need to verbally correct, critique, or—dare I say—criticize another?

Well, yes. We're all human. We make mistakes and get things wrong. And in many cases the only way to stop this from continuing to happen is to point it out. If one of your employees constantly shows up late at work, you would not be doing your job if you kept quiet about it.

Overhear one of your representatives unintentionally providing incorrect information to a customer? To not help her communicate more accurately would be harmful to every person involved with your company, employees and customers alike.

What about your business associate who overpaid on a negotiable product? Or your customer who is demanding increasingly more than what was agreed upon (often called "scope creep"), which is becoming more and more burdensome every day?

And if one of your children is breaking an important rule, obviously, correction is in order.

The real question then is not, is there a need to do so, but rather, is it possible to correct someone in a way that will lead them to not only accept your suggestion without becoming defensive but to truly embrace it and act in a way that corrects their behavior?

Yes, so long as you keep the human ego in mind and realize the key is tact.

"But, It's for Their Own Good!"

People often ask why others have such a difficult time accepting constructive criticism. One of my blog readers wrote: "Whether I'm correcting my children or employees, I feel as though they always have a negative reaction to what I say. This disturbs me. When I correct, it's only for their own good and to help them to become more effective. Is there something I'm missing here? Why are they so resistant to my helping them?"

I appreciate his question because it shows a real desire to understand and implement a more productive way of communicating with people he cares about.

As we learned in section four, whether or not people buy into what we say typically depends less upon logic than on how their ego accepts what they hear.

And this is why they seem to resist corrections, critique, help, and advice. Yes, even when it's for their own good!

Wouldn't you agree that, generally speaking, few people truly enjoy being corrected or criticized? I mean, I can't think of the last time someone criticized or corrected me—even nicely—and I responded by saying, "*Thank you! Thank you* for pointing out the error of my ways."

The Most Powerful Word in the English Language

As related earlier, I learned years ago both from listening to and watching my Dad that "tact is the language of strength." When words, requests, and suggestions are phrased and communicated tactfully, people are open. When not, they aren't.

While at first you will have to work at remaining conscious about utilizing tact, it will soon become a natural part of your being. And you're going to love the results!

The first step to utilizing tact is simply to think before you speak. Consider what you are going to say . . . before you say it. Edit your *speech before* you speak. Actually ask yourself the question, *How will he or she feel regarding what I'm about to say, and how I'm about to say it?*

You'll accomplish that by first controlling your own emotions.

The second step is to utilize the correct words, in the correct way that will honor the other person's belief system, their ego, and the emotions accompanying their ego.

In order to improve quickly, critique yourself after conversations. *Did I think before I spoke? Was I considerate of their feelings? Was I gentle in my manner? Did I provide a positive frame? Was the expression on my face consistent with my words?*

The exact words you use are not as important as the attitude behind them, though the correct words are indeed very important. When you begin with the right intent, the right words will generally follow. Again, this is the main reason why we include empathy right along with tact. Empathy often determines the attitude.

Here are just a few quick examples of tactful replies.

"Susan, thank you so much for this information. While it doesn't fit with the direction we're looking to go in, please know how much we appreciate you bringing it to our attention."

"Tom, that's a very reasonable thought and something to definitely consider. For my own clarification, when you say you're concerned with delivery issues, is there something specific you're thinking of?"

"Sweetie, you worked so hard on your report. I'm very proud of you. If you could make it a little neater, I think the teacher

160

will be much more impressed and your chances of an excellent grade will be a lot better."

Review the above tactfully phrased statements and ask yourself what their untactful counterpart statements would sound like. Then compare the two and consider which way will help you be a much more effective and powerful influencer and persuader.

By the way, untactful doesn't necessarily mean "mean." It might be simply short and cold (or just not warm), without communicating consideration for the other person's feelings. That still hurts him and will not bring about the positive feelings you are intending. Whether nasty or simply neutral, neither works nearly as well as tact.

Tact truly is the language of strength.

THE BEAUTY OF EMPATHY

A well-developed sense of empathy is key to your mastery of Ultimate Influence. It's that important. The good news is that—as with other principles—even if empathy is not a trait or skill you come by naturally, it can be developed. This is true whether you are trying to understand why someone is resistant to your viewpoint or attempting to help them through an issue or difficult time.

I believe that in any relationship—business or personal—empathy (the ability to identify with another's feelings) is a key differentiator between the successful and the unsuccessful. Those who have the talent and skill, both at having empathy and, just as important, being able to *communicate* empathy, are at a huge advantage over those who don't.

At times we might actually be able to identify or know what and/ or how they are feeling. If so, communicate that. Keep in mind that while understanding how they feel is important, it's not enough. The key is to *communicate* that you understand how they feel.

Even If You Don't Relate, Communicate!

Understanding is the goal, but what if you really can't relate? Let's face it: there are times when not only do we not know *exactly* how someone else feels, we have absolutely *no idea* how he or she feels.

Yet we can still be empathetic. As mentioned earlier, communicating empathy doesn't necessarily mean you actually feel what the other person feels. The truth is you might not. It *does* mean you communicate that you understand they are feeling *something*.

In a Facebook discussion I once started about empathy, Pastor Tom Sims from Clovis, California, wrote: "There is always something inside of us, some memory of personal pain or struggle that unites us in a common humanity and enables us to relate in compassion."

Wow. That is powerful!

When someone with empathy listens, the other person feels truly heard. And even just feeling heard is what often makes the difference between helpless and hope, between discouragement and determination to overcome something difficult.

Empathy Versus Sympathy

I've always loved Zig Ziglar's explanation regarding the difference between empathy and sympathy. With empathy, while you identify with and feel for the other person, you are still able to be part of the solution and help. With sympathy, you identify so strongly that you become part of the problem and are not able to help.

To illustrate the difference, he used the example of being on a cruise ship and encountering someone suffering from seasickness.

If you have empathy, you make them comfortable, get a washcloth for them, perhaps get some seasickness pills, and call for the ship's doctor.

If you have sympathy, you identify *so* strongly with their problem that you become seasick yourself and you're no good either to them *or* to yourself.

I thought this idea was also explained nicely in Tim Sanders's excellent book, *The Likeability Factor*. Tim points out a significant difference between the two in terms of focus.

> If you are sympathetic to others, your heart goes out to them and you feel compassion, but these are *your* feelings. You don't know what *they're* feeling. You're not trying to know. You're simply feeling bad that others feel bad (or lonely, or depressed, or angry).

> If you are empathetic to others, however, you are not merely feeling sorry for them but are projecting yourself into their hearts, as though you are sensing what it's like to be in their shoes.

In other words, sympathy is about you, while empathy is about them.

So while sympathy is certainly admirable, and there is a definite time and place for it, it's not necessarily where the focus should be. If we truly want to provide value to the other person, empathy is much more productive because it means our focus is on them. And that's where it should be.

46

LEAD-IN PHRASES PAVE THE WAY

Many people have a huge challenge with accepting advice and direction. Yet, in the real world, if they're not doing the right things, or they're not doing things right, they need to be helped, guided, and persuaded to do so.

How do you do this without offending them and causing resistance, and in a way that helps them to not only accept but even embrace your suggestion? One very helpful method is using what I call lead-in phrases. Utilized as a way to communicate both tact and empathy, they are simple to use and work like magic.

A lead-in is a short phrase that softens or buffers the potential sting of your advice and makes it more acceptable and easier to embrace. Simply use these before the advice you provide.

Here are a few examples of suggestions with successful lead-ins, which are in italics.

> "Steve, *I might be wrong about this,* why don't we try putting the widget here?"
>
> "Shirley, *this is just a thought.* I'm wondering if perhaps the whichamahoozee would be more cost-effective if we . . ."

"Ron, *I'm wondering,* what if we were to change one part of
the presentation to . . . ?"

"*This is my opinion only,* Patti. Having Tom run this particular unit could be a good first step in helping him become a more effective leader."

"Donna, *it seems to me, and I could very well be wrong,* is the
timing of this launch just a bit too late to . . . ?"

And this one will practically always cause the person to be more
receptive:

"Joe, *you know more about this than I do.* I'm wondering if . . ."

Many master persuaders become adept at using lead-in phrases
whenever and to whomever they offer advice. Let's face it, sometimes
the pill is simply easier to swallow if it's mixed into the applesauce.

There are two major benefits to using lead-ins.

1. **To open their minds.** Yes, it makes your opinion or suggestion more
   palatable. As you know, a person's ego will often stand in the way
   of their being receptive to another's idea. The above phrases act as
   buffers to their ego. In other words, you are not saying, I'm right
   and you are wrong. Instead, you are allowing for the definite possibility that you might not be correct.

   The interesting effect is that far from causing the other person
   to doubt the truth of your statement, it will actually cause them to
   be a lot more open to it.

   Counterintuitive? Yes. Effective? Absolutely!

2. **To open your mind.** Another benefit of these phrases is that they
   cause us to ask ourselves if we are, in fact, correct. This way, we
   keep ourselves from making more incorrect statements than we
   otherwise might, and develop the reputation with others that
   when we do speak up, we tend to know what we are talking about.

47

DEFLECTION VIA THE PARRY

n chapter 39 we discussed the profound influence and persuasive abilities of Abraham Lincoln. He knew how to keep conflict to a minimum and turn adversaries into allies. The following is an excellent example that I read somewhere a long time ago.

> [On one occasion] when another official sharply criticized Lincoln's judgment, the president responded to a reporter's interrogation by saying he had great respect for the other man, and if this official had concerns about him, there must be some truth to it. Such discretion disarmed divisiveness that was intended to draw Lincoln into side-skirmishes, it won the hearts of his friends and foes and it allowed Lincoln to maintain focus on more important issues.

By doing this, Lincoln utilized the tactic of deflection. This means to softly parry a strong challenge or accusation, deflecting it into another direction where it is now harmless.

If you watch a boxing match you'll notice that when one fighter throws a jab (a straight punch, usually with the left hand), the intended target will, very coolly, wait until the punch almost hits him and then redirect it with his right hand by using a very slight flick of the wrist. The rub is that the harder the punch is thrown, the less effort it takes to deflect it and render it harmless.

When someone says something to you, or about you, your instinct is to fight back. But that won't accomplish the results you're really after—making the insult or the insulter disappear. It will typically have just the opposite effect of drawing you more heavily into the confrontation and providing fodder for the conflict. Instead, do what Lincoln did. Compliment the offender and leave him and his comment without the power to hurt you. You can do this in one of two ways.

1. **Acknowledge the source positively.** If you're told what someone said about you then, like Lincoln, express your admiration for that person and suggest that, "If Pat said it, it's something I should at least look into."

   This parry will disarm the person who just related Pat's words. He or she cannot argue with you, because you did not argue with them. They can't debate the point, because you've politely refused to debate. And (perhaps most important) they cannot quote your defensive response to anyone else, including Pat, because you did not respond defensively.

   If you can do it with authenticity, begin as Lincoln did by saying, "I have great respect for Doug." That will only make you look better. If that is not something you're comfortable with, it isn't necessary. The key is that you don't get down to Doug's level but stay above it. You might instead say, "While I don't see that as being the case, I try and be open to suggestions and improvement. It's something I'll definitely take time and consider." You didn't exactly edify Doug, but you didn't disrespect him, either.

2. **Acknowledge the critique.** If a person criticizes you directly, acknowledge to the person that he or she may just have a point and it's something you need to consider. If that's not appropriate, simply thank them for bringing it up. You can then decide whether a

further response or explanation is necessary. An excellent parry, or deflection, is to simply say, "That's a good question" or "You make a valid point."

Please understand and keep in mind that I'm not advising you to become a doormat. Nor am I suggesting that you not answer or stick up for yourself. Taking a definite position might be necessary. What the deflection does, however, is keep it *impersonal*. It allows for *positive detachment* so that your answer can best serve everyone and not simply reflect negative or hurt feelings.

Here are three ways that you can develop your ability in this regard.

- Practice parrying whenever you are confronted, regardless of the lightness or seriousness of the confrontation.
- Watch other people during their conflicts and observe how they handle a left jab. Do they deflect it with a classy parry, or do they get caught up in trying to stop the verbal punch? How does that work out for them?
- Watch interviews on television and observe the dynamic. Note the ones who seem most efficient in the art of deflection, and determine to model them in future similar situations.

When you become proficient at this, you'll find it to be one of the most empowering (not to mention fun!) aspects of your interpersonal communications . . . and your ability to influence others.

48

KIND WORDS REGARDING YOUR COMPETITORS

The story about Abraham Lincoln in the previous chapter is a great reminder that it is a good idea to speak well not only of your adversaries but of your direct competitors, as well. Rarely will it come back to haunt you, and it could go a long way in making you look even better in the eyes of your prospects.

Indeed, most salespeople have been correctly taught never to speak ill of their competition. Doing so will only make them look bad. Unfortunately, most salespeople have been taught not to say anything *good* about their competition, either. I disagree with this counsel and have found just the opposite to be effective in my sales career.

Whenever I'm speaking with a prospect and they bring up one of my competitors, I go out of my way to say something nice about him or her. Why? It's not because I'm a nice guy (though, I'd like to think I am).

The reason is that by complimenting my competitor, I'm actually building up *myself* in the mind of my prospect. If your prospect brings up the name of your competitor and you speak highly of them, what does that tell your prospect about *you*?

1. **You are confident.** You must have a lot of confidence to speak highly of this person without fear that you're helping their business or hurting yours.

2. **You are successful.** If you are confident, you also must be successful. After all, unsuccessful people don't have that type of confidence in themselves.

3. **You are safe.** If you pass up an opportunity to criticize your competition, your prospect knows they never have to worry about you saying anything negative about them or their staff either.

   Obviously, if you know for sure that your competitor is a thief, you can't lie and speak well of them. In that case, be sure and say nothing at all. But, that aside, if you can possibly say something nice about him or her, do so. It will only reflect well on you.

49

TACT DOES NOT EQUAL COMPROMISE

Whether we're discussing this within the context of a debate, a corporate negotiation, or a simple transaction between a buyer and a seller, the principle holds true: tact and compromise are not the same thing.

This is not to say that compromise is never appropriate. Without question, it is often a vital ingredient in getting along and working with others day-to-day. However, when it's important to stand by your decision and not compromise, you can still disagree without being disagreeable.

Yes, being polite, being gracious, being kind and tactful does not mean you agree with that person; nor does it signify you will cave in. While it's fine to negotiate or compromise on things, it is not okay to cave on our principles and beliefs.

My friend MaryKay Morgan wrote: *"One never has to let go of graciousness and good manners even in 'tough' negotiations."*

How true. In fact, I've always found that the more you maintain these good manners, the more successful you are likely to be in accomplishing your goal. When you maintain your sense of tact and kindness, the other person will be less inclined to maintain their defensive shield. And at that point change can occur.

Stay true to your principles, and don't lose your class.

GIVE THEM A BACK DOOR

B ob, there's a cat out there that looks like it hasn't eaten in days."
Those words were from my neighbor, Terry. So I went out to take
a look and, indeed, about fifty yards away, unsuccessfully hiding
in the bushes was a beautiful little stray cat. She was very skinny and
somewhat angry looking.

Refusing to even take water in a paper bowl while we were close
by, we left it there for her and, eventually, she drank from it.

Next, I tried to feed her some cat kibble. While I was nearby, she
wanted nothing to do with it. However, when I walked away, she
would come out to eat.

Hmm, I wondered if I could, in time, get close enough to feed her.
So I began to place the bowl closer and closer to my house. And as
long as I didn't get too close and she knew she had room to escape,
she'd eat. Within a week she came onto my patio to eat, so long as I
was on the other side of the glass door, and the patio door itself was
left ajar. In fact, as the cat would eat, she'd continually look back,
keeping her eye on the open back door.

A week later she actually came inside to eat, staying right at the edge of the open glass door. She'd even let me stand at the door near her, as long as I kept it open.

Then I decided to try to close the door and see if she would stay inside with me for a while. I wanted to do it slowly so as not to upset her. I had decided that I was falling in love with this little creature; I wanted her to be my cat, and I wanted to be her human.

I'd had no prior training with cats. As mentioned earlier, while I love all animals, I am a dog person (perhaps a dog fanatic is more accurate), and growing up, my family always had dogs. So I really didn't know what to expect, or if this was even going to work.

As I began to slowly slide the door closed, she stopped eating, turned her head, and looked as though she were about to dart out the door to safety. But before she did, I quickly opened it as wide as it would go. She then relaxed and continued eating.

After a couple more tries, I was able to close the door. She was fine. Now two years later, she is my faithful and loving companion (as much as a cat will allow herself to be). She is a great friend and terrific company. She lets me feed her, give her catnip, and scratch her behind her ears . . . *when* she is in the mood, of course.

She did write a somewhat unflattering blog post* about me while I was off speaking one weekend (how she got on to the Internet I still haven't figured out), but aside from that she's been a joy.

The point of the story is this: Liberty never wanted to leave. She just wanted to know she *could* leave. So long as she had a "back door" to escape out of, she was fine.

What About Two-Leggeds?

Our sales prospects, as well as anyone and everyone we are attempting to influence in any context of life, feel the same way.

---

* You can read her post at http://www.burg.com/2011/10/guest-post-by-me-liberty-the-cat.

They don't necessarily want to say no. They just want to know they *can* say no.

"You may or may not be interested."

"Is this a good time to speak, or have I caught you at a really awful time?"

"This isn't for everyone."

"Please don't feel obligated in any way."

Those are pretty counterintuitive statements. And they're very effective. Why?

When faced with potential conflict, people often feel pressured to respond or behave a certain way. This puts them on the defensive and creates an adversarial frame. In short, it makes them feel that if you win, they lose.

Thankfully, there's a pretty easy way to fix this.

If you want someone to take a certain action but don't want them to feel like they're being forced or manipulated into it, the best thing to do is communicate very clearly to them that they don't have to take that action.

In other words, give them an out (or, as Liberty would call it, a back door). This is a way of letting a person feel comfortable with you and the situation by providing them with an emotional escape route. This removes any pressure—even self-inflicted pressure—they might feel, because now they know they have a choice.

While human nature dictates that people will resist most of that which is forced upon them, it's also true that the greater the level of choice one has, the less he or she feels the need to *exercise* that choice.

To put it another way . . .

The bigger the out you give someone to take, the less they'll feel the need to take it.

Often used in the selling process, the out can be applied in practically any aspect of persuasion.

When the ticket agent at the airport could not find the notification waiving the extra fee, as had been promised, I utilized all of the first four of the principles discussed in the book. Of course, I was also very tactful and empathetic and I could tell she genuinely wanted to come through for me.

Unfortunately, she was having trouble locating the information she needed and it seemed as though she was considering giving up. I knew the time was just right to take the pressure off by giving her an out. So I told her: "If you can't do it, I'll definitely understand."

This is one of the most powerful out phrases you can ever use. Say these eight words, and you're almost guaranteed to move someone to your side of an issue.

If need be (and need probably *won't* be), you can follow up by gently saying, "If you could, I'd certainly appreciate it." Then, if need still be (which I can practically guarantee it won't), you finish with, "Of course, don't get yourself in any hot water over it."

You have honored this person by removing pressure and giving him or her the option to escape through the back door. This is far more successful than painting them into a corner where their ego will need to prevail. You've also just gently challenged them to come through and do their best, while assuring them that they are worth more to you as people than whether they can deliver what you want.

You might be wondering whether giving them this choice sets you up to be told no.

Please understand:

> You are not giving them the out so they will take it. Your goal is to make them feel comfortable enough not to feel the need to take it.

Of course, if they feel it is in their best interest to leave through the back door, they will. But they would have anyway. Or had they instead capitulated to your demands because they felt pressured to do so, they would have had to either go back on their word or perhaps sabotage the process.

Let it be their decision and—if they make the decision to proceed— they will feel good about it because it was *their* decision, not yours.

And the best way to increase the odds of them deciding to do what you are asking them to do is to make the option for them *not* to do it very clear.

HOW TO SAY NO GRACIOUSLY
AND EFFECTIVELY

Have you ever been asked to do something that you simply didn't want to do? Yet, saying no was difficult. On one hand, you didn't want to let someone down or even appear selfish.

On the other hand, you really didn't want to say yes.

You may have read an article or received advice saying that it's okay to just tell people no! Or, that "No" is a complete sentence. I've been at seminars where that advice was dispensed and saw the heads nod up and down in agreement. Well, despite the momentary feeling of empowerment that advice may bring you, saying no—especially like that—is much easier said than done.

After all, are you willing to say no in such a way that it offends a person, turns them off, closes the door on other opportunities, or simply runs contrary to your core value of treating people kindly?

Probably not. Especially if you're already the kind of person who has a hard time turning people down in the first place. So here's the good news: you *can* say no. And you can do it with tact, kindness, diplomacy, and in a way that makes the other person feel good about themselves.

So how exactly do you do this?

Let's use the very generic situation in which a person asks you to serve on a committee and, for whatever reason, it's not a position you'd like to take. Simply say: "Thank you so much for your kind offer. While it's not something I'd like to do, please know how honored I am to be asked."

Depending on what is more congruent with your personal style, you might substitute "I choose" for "I'd like," and "grateful" for "honored."

The key is to say it with kindness and gratitude and with absolutely *no* defensiveness.

Speaking of key points, there is one more. This is vital.

Make No Excuses!

Do not make an excuse for saying no!

Please resist the very natural urge to say, "I don't have time" or "I'm really not qualified," or anything similar you might be tempted to say. If you do, they'll attempt to answer your *objection* in order to persuade you. And when they overcome the objection, you'll either be cornered into accepting (so that you don't appear to be a liar) or you'll have to admit that what you said wasn't really true. You'll lose face, they'll resent you, you'll feel resentful of the situation, and feel badly about yourself.

So don't get sucked into that game. A simple answer such as the one above, along with a genuine smile, will accomplish your goal. That, and no excuses!

Will this work *every* time? Actually, yes, so long as you maintain your polite, grateful, yet steady "no thank you" posture.

For example, if they persist and say, "Oh, c'mon; why not?" or "Please, we really need you," all you have to do is reply with a sincere smile and say, "I'd just rather not, but thank you *so much* for considering me."

The person will understand that you're not going to accept the position, but cannot possibly be offended because of your gracious, humble, and appreciative attitude.

Once you begin training the people in your life (even those who are used to your giving in) that you are able to say no and not be bullied, coerced, or *guilted* into doing something, you will find that, from that point on, all it will take is one no per request not to be asked again.

Of course there are plenty of times that "Yes" is the correct and appropriate response. But saying no when you should say no allows you to say yes more often when you should say yes.

And it allows you to do what you say yes to much more effectively.

DON'T TREAD ON ME

Recall that earlier in the book we said that tact, kindness, and respect should never be confused with allowing yourself to be taken advantage of.

It's up to you, then, to ensure that while you deal fairly, ethically, and respectfully with others, that they do the same.

But what *if* the person you are dealing with doesn't follow this philosophy? One might advise, "Just don't do business with that person or company." That's fine in theory. And perhaps one day—when you can pick and choose with whom you do business—it will be fine in practice.

For most, however, and for a variety of reasons, working within these situations is a necessity.* It's also good for personal growth. After all, people are who they are. Learn and grow from them.

Three suggestions when dealing with disrespectful or possibly less-than-forthright people:

---

* Naturally, if this other person or company is simply dishonest, doing anything illegal, or taking advantage of others, then of course you would not do business with them. That is not what we are talking about here.

1. **Maintain your class.** Continue to operate from a high level of thought, action, and integrity. Stay polite and scrupulously honest. And as the late Dr. Stephen Covey said, "Win/Win or no deal." That's right, even if that's not a high value for them, it *is* for you.

2. **Refuse that which could harm you.** Say no with politeness and tact when what is being proposed or offered is not in your best and highest interest. Do this not with anger but with the kind of language, framing, and phrasing we've been discussing.

3. **Stay alert.** If, for whatever reason, you feel they cannot be trusted, then don't trust them. While typically I would say not to let on, there are certain situations in which you must tactfully (tactfully!) communicate this. You'll need to be the judge of that.

Tactfully Communicating Distrust

In responding to a request or call for inappropriate action you might say, "I'm not comfortable with . . . ," or use other "I messages" that communicate the point without causing a confrontation.

You could also say, "John, unfortunately, as much as I enjoy the idea that we can do business together, I don't get the feeling that you are as interested in a win/win for both of us." He'll definitely get the picture but is less likely to be offended because of the way you said it.

Yes, life is life and we need to know how to turn all types of potential adversaries into allies. Pull them up to your level if you can. If not, you can still protect yourself and your reputation while providing the exceptional value you always provide.

53

TURNING DOWN AN OFFER, WHILE LEAVING ROOM FOR ANOTHER

Imagine you want to buy a product but it either costs more than you're willing to spend or another aspect of the sale is unacceptable. How do you turn it down without offending the salesperson and keep the door open to further dialogue and negotiation?

Doing this correctly is vital; first, because treating people with dignity and respect is simply the right thing to do. And, as we've been discussing, the most effective way to obtain what you desire is to make the other person feel good about themselves, as well as about you.

The ego elicits emotional decisions and, if insulted, people will often make decisions that aren't even in their best interests. Yes, even salespeople. They might want the sale but typically not enough to allow themselves to feel abused.

One rude and counterproductive way of refusing an offer is by saying, "There's no way I'll accept that. You *must* give me . . . or I'm walking!" This removes the out or back door (see chapter 50) and paints the other person into a corner, where they must either walk away or capitulate.

On the other hand, you can very pleasantly turn down an offer while allowing that person to save face and still understand they need to come back with a better offer.

Consider an example.

Salesman Steve: "This is the price for the widget, and delivery will be in two weeks."

You: "Thank you, Steve. I appreciate the offer. Unfortunately, at that price and with the long delivery time, I can't justify making the purchase. But I *do* appreciate the offer."

Look at how tactfully you've framed this: you thanked him and expressed gratitude for his offer. You gave him the reasons you have to turn it down using a wonderful "I message." (Unlike when saying no graciously, in this case it is imperative to cite specific reasons in order to communicate the issue so he has the needed information to—if possible—be able to help you.) And then you once again expressed appreciation.

You've kindly and respectfully said no, while leaving his self-esteem intact. People like Steve *want* to do business with people like you. Now, say nothing and see if Steve comes back with another offer or asks you what price and/or delivery time would work better for you.

He probably will do just that. But what if he doesn't? There's a very simple and respectful question you can then ask him.

If, after a few seconds, he says nothing (and assuming you really want the widget enough to pursue this), simply ask: "Steve, what can you offer that would help me justify the decision to buy?"

That one question, asked with respect, will allow him to provide you with the appropriate answer.

He'll either come back with something better, or he won't. There's no guarantee he will. (Sometimes it's a condition, not a choice, meaning that he has no room to negotiate further.) The choice will then be yours.

However, what I can guarantee is that if you'll proceed with the "I couldn't justify" response as opposed to a simple "No," the odds of him going out of his way to make you happy will increase dramatically.

54

DEALING WITH AN INTERRUPTER

Have you ever been in a discussion with someone who constantly interrupted you? Frustrating, isn't it? You want to make a point, but they are so passionate about their view, they interrupt you the very moment they hear a word or phrase with which they disagree.

If you're not careful, and you allow yourself to get caught up in a back-and-forth pattern of interrupting one another, the disagreement will escalate into a shouting match. The result? Neither side will have heard or been heard, and bad feelings between you will ensue. It will also make it that much harder for you to influence that person the next time.

So how do you handle this touchy, aggravating, and potentially explosive situation?

One effective maneuver works well after the person has interrupted several times. And especially when he's interrupted after asking you a challenging question.

First, wait until he finishes his thought and then calmly and politely say, "Dave, while I appreciate your feelings about this topic, it doesn't do *either* of us any good if you interrupt me while I'm trying to answer the question that *you* asked me."

In other words, don't try to continue your initial response but wisely establish the new precedent, implying that if the person is interested in continuing this discussion, the only way it can happen is to listen without interrupting.

As you may have recognized, you've now tactfully *reframed* the pattern of the conversation.

A second method is to simply stop talking and allow the person to finish their thought. Then, without any sign of emotion or frustration (that is key), continue with your original thought. Do this enough and there's a good chance that the other person will get the point—although you are polite, you refuse to be thrown off track.

A third way to respond to interruptions—in this case, those involving rapid-fire questions during a disagreement—is to simply say, "Would you like me to finish my first thought or answer the question you just asked?" Then, without hesitating and with a genuinely humble, self-effacing smile, add, "Actually, I'm not smart enough to keep all this information in my head. I can only answer one question at a time."

Understand that at times you'll face a person who really doesn't want to hear your viewpoint. Their mind is made up and they wish *not* to be confused by the facts. They'll often seem like a prosecuting attorney just waiting for you to slip up before going in for the kill.

In this case, you might decide to slow down even more, remain very calm, and perhaps even ask, with an "I message," "Dave, are you genuinely interested in my thoughts on this? I feel sort of like your mind might already be made up about this issue. I'd love to answer you and have the opportunity to learn from you as well, but I also need to feel as though I can express my point."

The key, as always, is to respond and not react. Think first. Ask yourself, *What is it that I want to derive from the conversation?* And what does the other person want, as well? Then making the right moves becomes easy.

Combining a respectful approach along with an understanding that, more than likely, he or she does not want to offend you but is simply excited about their point of view, you'll enjoy the process and be most effective. You'll also be able to emotionally detach from the outcome. That—of course—will make you all the more effective.

It's also very important to make sure *you* are not the guilty party.

This should go without saying, but you cannot be an influencer and an interrupter* at the same time. So if Ultimate Influence is your goal, and *if* interrupting is a habit of yours, the time to break it is now.

This was a bad habit of mine for a long time. Once I became aware of its destructive nature, it became my mission to stop.

How? Focus, concentration, and practice. *Lots* of practice!

I made it my primary purpose in a conversation not to interrupt. I put sticky notes with this reminder on my telephone, around my house, on my computer, everywhere and anywhere I might see it.

I failed, succeeded, and failed again. And then, amazingly enough, the times I'd interrupt became more and more rare.

For me, interrupting is now mainly a thing of the past. I still do it occasionally. However, now *I catch myself* and can immediately apologize. This honors the other person, acknowledges my error, and reminds me not to do that for the remainder of the conversation.

You can do the same and it's well worth the effort. Practically nothing else will stymie one's ability to lead, to influence, to persuade, and to effectively communicate as will interrupting others. They will become frustrated, annoyed, angry, and be less inclined to buy into your ideas. Also, it simply makes it harder for them to like you.

Overcome this habit and people will credit you as a great listener. That's one compliment I never used to receive, and now I often do just because I broke one *very* counterproductive habit.

---

* Actual term: *Interruptus Maximus Obnoxius.*

THE BEN FRANKLIN METHOD FOR WINNING PEOPLE OVER

n Benjamin Franklin's *The Autobiography and Other Writings*, the inventor, statesman, and diplomat tells of an incident with a man who opposed his reelection as clerk of the General Assembly of the Pennsylvania House.

Although he managed to keep the office, Franklin knew that this person, whom he described as "a gentleman of fortune and education with talents that were likely to give him, in time, great influence in the House," could be trouble later on. He aimed to ensure that didn't happen by "making, of an enemy, a friend."

Let's let Ben tell us how he did it.

> I did not, however, aim at gaining his favour by paying any servile respect to him, but after some time took this other method. Having heard that he had in his library a certain very scarce and curious book, I wrote a note to him expressing my desire of perusing that book and requesting he would do me the favour of lending it to me for a few days.

He sent it immediately—and I returned it in about a week with another note expressing strongly my sense of the favour. When we next met in the House, he spoke to me (which he had never done before), and with great civility. And he ever afterward manifested a readiness to serve me on all occasions, so that we became great friends, and our friendship continued to his death.

Here, the man known as Gentle Ben goes on to explain the principle.

This is another instance of the truth of an old maxim I had learned, which says, "He that has once done you a kindness will be more ready to do you another than he whom you yourself have obliged." And it shows how much more profitable it is prudently to remove, than to resent, return, and continue inimical proceedings.

Yes, it's intuitive to believe that reaching out and doing something of value for the other person first would begin the healing process. And indeed it is often very effective. But Franklin's reversal is powerful and shows how taking the very *opposite* approach can also bring excellent results.

Tact doesn't always have to do with the exact words you speak. Sometimes it's just a matter of determining what will most effectively help another person adjust their attitude, thoughts, and feelings.

What Franklin said in his final sentence makes a whole lot of sense. To paraphrase: we're better off making a friend than keeping an enemy.

Or turning adversaries into allies! (You knew that was coming, didn't you?)

DR. FRANKLIN AND ANOTHER GREAT LESSON IN COMMUNICATION

We've discussed lead-in phrases that help soften the blow when attempting to influence or persuade someone to your side of an issue.

Related to this is the idea that anything we say can be communicated more effectively and persuasively by not coming across in a dogmatic, know-it-all fashion but, instead, with the humility of one who honors the feelings and opinions of others.

This reminds me of another terrific teaching of Benjamin Franklin, also from his autobiography.

Although, through logic, Franklin could practically always outmaneuver his *adversary,* he soon realized that doing so did not result in their having good feelings toward him, but just the opposite. And while he might convince them, he would often not persuade them. After all, they felt put down and insulted; their ego would not allow them to admit defeat and a change of opinion.

According to Dr. Franklin:

I gradually left [this method], retaining only the habit of expressing myself in terms of modest diffidence. I never used, when I advanced, anything that may possibly be disputed—the words, "certainly," "undoubtedly," or any others that give the air of positiveness to an opinion. Rather, I'd say, "I conceive or apprehend a thing to be so or so," "It appears to me," or "I should think it so or so, for such and such reasons," or "I imagine it to be so," or "It is so if I am not mistaken."

This habit, I believe, has been of great advantage to me when I have had occasion to inculcate my opinions and persuade men into measures that I have been from time to time engaged in promoting.

So let's take an important lesson from the great diplomat and express ourselves with humility and tact.

"The Fact of the Matter Is . . . It's Just My Opinion"

I loved Franklin's term regarding words that "give the air of positiveness to an opinion." I catch myself doing that far too often. On the phone recently, I heard myself saying, "The fact of the matter is," before making my point.

I quickly realized three things.

1. It wasn't necessarily a factual statement. It was just my opinion.
2. Even *if* what I said was correct, leading with those six words was most likely going to cause resistance in the listener rather than acceptance.
3. Most people (in my opinion only) who begin spouting their opinion by saying things such as, "The fact of the matter

is," typically follow those words with something that is incorrect.

So when you wish to influence others by communicating a point
in the most persuasive way, you might want to take Ben Franklin's
advice and begin with something like, "In my opinion."

But, of course, that's just . . . well, you know.

TIMING RULES!

've often talked about—in other books, my blog, and at my live presentations—the importance of saying the right thing to the right person. This is often discussed within the context of selling where even the best positive persuasion skills are useless if the person you're persuading doesn't have the authority to agree to your offer. The same holds true in many different areas.

But, there's another element that is also easy to miss. And that is the timing.

While it's important to say the right thing to the right person, you must also say it *at the right time*.

Consider these examples of bad timing.

> She is talking to someone and might not appreciate your jumping in with your own agenda.
>
> He has just finished a difficult conversation. Facial expression indicates he is not in a helpful mood.
>
> You are in the middle of a noisy room.
>
> You have only a few minutes and this is something that might require a longer discussion.

So keep time in mind. If the timing is not right and it's something that can be discussed later, set a time to do so. If the conversation must take place now, first acknowledge that you understand the timing is not perfect. Assure her that if the situation wasn't critical, you would not even think of bringing this up to her right now.

Then, utilizing the information we are discussing in this book, go ahead and say the right thing to that right person.

It's important to be sure and schedule enough time for any important conversation. Taking it a step further, I suggest that:

> When you are about to take part in an important conversation, be sure that all parties have the time and willingness to participate.

This sounds both simple and self-evident, yet it is a crucial element that, when overlooked, can come back to bite you.

Consider the following scenario in which you have something important to say to your supervisor Tom.

YOU: "Do you have some time to talk? It's kind of important."

TOM: "I've got some time but have to head out in a little while. What do you need?"

YOU: "Oh, that's okay. I'll wait until you have more time."

TOM: "No, really, go ahead; I'm fine. What's up?"

Now confident you have his attention, you begin. But you notice that as you're speaking, he looks at his watch every so often. His engagement level is sort of low and he's beginning to unconsciously shuffle some papers. Eventually, he gives a very hurried and unsatisfying response to the issue you brought up, assuring you that he gets the point and *blah, blah, blah.*

But he didn't get the point. And you most likely regret having had this very abridged conversation. You sense the result is not going to be what you were hoping for.

Whether holding a family meeting or having a very necessary one-on-one discussion with a loved one, whether needing to speak with your boss about an important issue, having a staff conference, or setting an appointment with a sales prospect, establish that the time is there and available.

Before the conversation or meeting ever begins, be sure all parties are committed to the process, and for the amount of time that has been agreed upon.

Gently create agreement for sufficient time. How?

1. **Ask for it.** If this is a family or group, you might say, "I'd like for us to discuss . . . and I believe it's going to take up to forty-five minutes. Do you have forty-five minutes that you can dedicate without feeling pressed for time?"

   If it's a boss, it might be, "Ms. Thomas, I need to discuss an important issue. Could we talk for about fifteen minutes? That's about how much time I believe we'll need."

2. **Be able to work around a curveball.** Ms. Thomas says, "I really only have a couple minutes until my next meeting, but please go ahead. I'm sure I'll be able to help with whatever the problem might be."

Here's where you need to tactfully use the right words.

YOU: "I appreciate that, Ms. Thomas. Thank you so much. Actually, I know I'll need about fifteen minutes. Could we reschedule for when you have a bit more time?"

MS. THOMAS: "Really, I'd prefer we discuss it now. I'm sure it'll be okay."

YOU: "I appreciate that so much. This is something that's really more than a two-minute conversation, though, and the last thing I want to do is waste two minutes of your time when I know that won't be enough. If we could, may I schedule a fifteen-minute block with your admin?"

Yes, we used "I" several times. In this case it's important to utilize an "I message" because you want to take the responsibility for needing more time. Putting the responsibility on them with a "you message" could make them feel defensive and be more inclined to insist on a "now" conversation.

Just like saying no graciously, it's vital to maintain inner strength and respond in a way that communicates you are honoring that person, even though you are not giving in to them.

Utilize this method whenever you need to make sure there is enough time for an effective conversation. Just remember that if you allow yourself to get sucked into a conversation when the proper amount of time has not been allocated for its success, you might as well not even bother. The results will most likely not be what you intended.

Understanding that will help you remain strong yet tactful in order to obtain the agreement of time you need.

MAKE PEOPLE COMFORTABLE
WITH YOU

Have you ever come face-to-face with someone who probably should have known your name but didn't? Could you sense their discomfort? If so, did you make it easier for them by reintroducing yourself by name, or did you make them stew in embarrassing discomfort?

Your answer probably reveals whether they felt good about you or not. It also tells whether, all things being equal, they'd choose to be your friend, do business with you, refer your services to others, or help you accomplish a goal.

Form the habit of reintroducing yourself to someone you've recently met, whenever you see them, until you are certain that they know your name (they might even let you know themselves). Doing this will never come back to haunt you, but could possibly make a very significant, positive difference in your current and future relationship with them.

The same goes for the telephone. I can't tell you how often I receive calls where the person says, "Hi, Bob, how are you?" without identifying himself or herself. Since I don't ever want to embarrass someone or make them feel unimportant, I say, "Great, how about you?"

Then I spend the next couple of minutes trying to figure out who I'm talking to.

When reaching someone on the telephone, I generally begin by saying, "Hi, Dave, this is Bob Burg." And I tend to do this until they tell me they recognize my voice and assure me the introduction is no longer necessary. It's obvious, however, that they appreciate the gesture.

Admittedly, at times I've taken this practice too far. I remember once calling a very nice woman and when she answered the phone I said, "Hi, this is Bob Burg." She responded by saying, "Bob, I think I know who you are by now—we've been dating for three months!" Oh well, moderation has never been my strongest suit.

You may feel a little embarrassed if you reintroduce yourself to someone who already knows who you are, but you'll never offend a person by showing them the courtesy of making life easier for them. On the other hand, you could embarrass them, make them uncomfortable, and even cause slight resentment if you don't.

Which is more desirable? And is it worth a tiny amount of extra effort?

A small part of developing Ultimate Influence? Maybe small. Maybe not so small.

59

COLLECTING MONEY OWED YOU IN A WINNING WAY

M ost people are uncomfortable talking about money. Perhaps they were raised to believe that discussing money with people they don't know very well is impolite.

And indeed, discussing money inappropriately can easily put people off. You've probably interacted with someone who constantly complained about not having enough money, making you feel uncomfortable, or bragged about how much they spent on a lavish vacation or object.

The trouble comes when someone owes you money but either forgets or is late in paying it back. Whether it's a roommate who owes you his part of the rent, a friend who borrowed a bit to get by, or a loyal customer who has fallen behind on a payment, in these cases you are faced with a dilemma: how do you get the person to pay you the money you're owed without offending them or ruining your relationship?

Usually it's enough to simply remind the person: "Sally, do you think you could give me your rent check tomorrow? I need to pay the landlord at the end of the week."

But what about more persistent situations? For example, collecting from a late-paying customer or client can be very unnerving. It's the very essence of a conflict you don't want to have.

I'm not referring to those who might simply have forgotten and have done so for the first time. When that is the case, just call and politely remind them. There shouldn't be a problem.

But what about collecting from those for whom—while it *seems* they will pay—it does not appear to be a priority. Perhaps you've been told the check is in the mail, but it hasn't arrived.

You've got that feeling in the pit of your stomach that:

1. You are going to be cheated out of the money owed after you've already completed the work or provided the product.
2. If you do collect, it will be the result of having to threaten, cajole, or in some other way ruin the relationship, and you'll lose their future business.

Regarding the second point, some might advise to simply avoid doing business again with that type of person. And in a perfect world that works. But maybe now you still need their business. So if you can both collect the money you are owed and retrain them to pay on time while continuing to do business with you, isn't that a better alternative?

Do you want to handle this successfully in the way of the Ultimate Influencer? Here's how to effectively and tactfully collect what is owed to you.

1. **Communicate the issue.** Compose a letter. This could be email or snail mail, depending upon how well you know them and their online habits.
2. **Be tactful.** Compliment their values and integrity.
3. **Show gratitude.** Express how much you enjoy serving them, and that you hope they feel the value you provide them exceeds what they pay.
4. **Have a call to action.** Let them know that it would "mean a lot" to you to receive payment today.
5. **Allow them to save face.** Add that if there is a problem you are not aware of, you'd appreciate their letting you know so you can discuss.

The key is not to be demanding but also not to come across as weak. A day after your initial request, follow up with a call and ask if a check has been sent. Assuming they actually do plan on paying you, this should work.

Let's look at a sample letter.

Dear Pat,

Thank you for your business. Aside from having an excellent product, you and your team embody the type of values based on a high degree of integrity.

It's an honor and pleasure for me to serve your _____ needs. As you know, our goal is to provide the ultimate customer experience and I sincerely hope that you feel that we deliver more in value to you than we take in payment. If that is ever not the case, I hope you will let me know directly and personally.

Pat, the payment of $675.00 for the latest project we did for you (invoice #5791-A, dated 6/20/13) is past due and it would mean a lot to me if you would have a check sent to us today. That way, we can continue to feel good about providing you and your excellent company with timely, value-based service.

Of course, if there is a problem I am not aware of, please call me right away at 555-1212 so we can discuss and determine the proper steps.

Again, thank you for your business, and best regards,

Don Thomas

Call Pat the next day to follow up. You may not have to. You might just receive an immediate email of apology with a promise that the check is being sent out today . . . and it will be.

60

THE PLEASURE OF "MY PLEASURE"

I remember years ago speaking for one of the Ritz Carlton properties and being so impressed when interacting with the guest-contact employees. The same holds true today.

Rather than saying "Hi" or "Hello" or, even worse, the non-greetings, "How are ya" or "How ya doin'" (notice the lack of question marks because neither are actually questions), they say—depending upon the time of day—"Good morning," "Good afternoon," or "Good evening."

And when a guest thanks them, their response is always gracious. What do you think they say? "No problem"?

No way!

They say, "My pleasure."

And this is what Ultimate Influencers say. It works anytime, anywhere, with anyone, and in practically any situation. The little things we say and do so often make a big difference in our abilities to influence others.

"My pleasure" says it all, doesn't it? It was my pleasure to help you and I will be happy to do so again anytime. On the other hand, responding with "No problem" implies just the opposite; it was sort of a hassle to help you, but I did it anyway. Not the message you want to deliver.

I was speaking to a class of high school seniors and suggested that whether working at a restaurant, running their own car detailing service, or interviewing for a job, they could separate themselves from the rest of the pack simply using those two words. "My pleasure!"

The same goes for adults.

"You're welcome" is good. "My pleasure" is even better.

My suggestion is to make this a habit. You won't regret it.

Glad to help. In fact, it's . . . (c'mon, say it with me).

DELIVER THE RIGHT MESSAGE
FOR YOUR AUDIENCE

While on the road speaking, I decided to visit a very nice, local health club to get in some exercise.

After about ten minutes on the treadmill, an announcement came over the loudspeaker. The message had a very condescending tone. And the words weren't much better: "Members, please show common courtesy by not staying on the cardio machines for more than thirty minutes at a time when there are people waiting. It's very rude to keep other members waiting."

Now, it was obvious to my observing eyes and ears that this immediately rankled many of those in the gym, not the least of those being the ones presently working out on the cardio machines.

Did the employee who made the announcement have a valid point? Sure, the thirty-minute time limit is very practical and, according to the regulars I spoke to, well accepted by all. If some people were not honoring that, it needed to be addressed. And a public announcement would, in fact, be quite appropriate in this case as a good reminder.

However, at the time of the announcement, only about 50 percent of the cardio machines were in use, which made the members a bit curious regarding the timing. Judging by the sarcastic laughter and shaking of heads, the gym goers were a bit perturbed by it as well.

Both the tone and the wording of the announcement were negative and insulting, as though the gym staff were addressing a bunch of irresponsible children, not paying members and loyal customers who could very easily take their membership fees elsewhere.

So how could the announcement have been more effectively worded and delivered so that the members accepted the rule and appreciated the reminder? Here's a suggestion:

> Attention members. Good morning. As always, we're glad to have you with us, and it's inspiring to see you working out so hard. Congratulations on your effort. Because we want to deliver an excellent [facility's name] workout experience, during those times when the cardio machines are at capacity, please be sure and not stay on more than thirty minutes. This will ensure that none of you will ever have to wait too long and you can get your workout in at your convenience. Thank you for your attention, and for being a member of [facility's name]. Have a great workout and a terrific day!

This message sets a positive frame and dramatically increases the odds that the message will not only be appreciated but adhered to. There's even a W.I.I.F.M. ("What's in it for me?") element for those listening: *as long as I respect this rule, I won't ever get stuck waiting too long for one of the machines.*

Same intent as the first message; much different results.

You can very quickly become proficient at crafting similar messages simply by paying attention to the often poor communication you experience and asking yourself how to make it more acceptable and persuasive.

Of course, you can also review the suggestions in this book whenever you feel you need a bit of a refresher.

SEEKING FORGIVENESS

At times we need to mend a rift, perhaps one we inadvertently caused. Often a simple yet heartfelt apology will suffice; other times it won't, and the person is not moved to forgive. An uncomfortable feeling, indeed.

One of my blog readers asked:

> What if you've apologized genuinely and the person won't relent, won't forgive, stays angry and won't acknowledge you—to the point of ignoring your attempts at email and phone calls? Then what? I can't cut off my arm or give up an organ. Where do you go from an honest, sincere, heartfelt apology? Unless staying angry is simply where she wants to stay? Any pearls of wisdom would be really appreciated. This could cost a budding friendship and I'd hate for that to happen.

I didn't know enough about the situation, about the writer or her friend, or about the context to know *exactly* what to tell this person. I'm always hesitant to provide a one-answer-fits-all type of response for this very reason.

That said, here are several suggestions I provided for her to consider.

- She might still be in her anger. In other words, she might still be too upset to be reasoned with.
- Have an intermediary, whom you both trust, try and intercede. If this is someone your friend respects, she may be apt to listen.
- Let your friend know, via any medium (telephone, voice mail, email, or in person), that you understand she is still angry and not yet ready to speak but that when she is, you'll be there for her.
- Some people do want to stay angry. If that's the case, you may have to emotionally detach yourself from the situation and just let her come to you, if that's what is supposed to happen.

Again, these are opinions based on very limited knowledge on my part of a very unique situation. I hope, however, that they at least provide some food for thought.

Remember, even Ultimate Influencers make mistakes. When that happens, be prepared to apologize with no excuses. Hopefully, your apology will be accepted. If not, you'll find the above to be both viable and productive options.

CHAPTER

63

"ACKNOWLEDGE ME!"

I was at a new diagnostic center for some blood work recently and witnessed an interesting exchange.

An elderly and somewhat perturbed woman approached the receptionist, who asked how she could help. The senior citizen, attempting to be cordial but assertive, said she was there "To take another test, as your company lost the first one. I can't believe I had to drive all the way back again because of a mistake like that."

The receptionist politely, but without *any* semblance of feeling or empathy, said, "Please fill out this form."

The woman, unacknowledged and dissatisfied, continued, with what was obviously defensive laughter, "I tell you, if it happens again, I'm through with this place. Imagine that happening—losing someone's information like that."

The receptionist, again politely, and again without *any* semblance of feeling or empathy, said, "Have a seat. Someone will be with you soon."

The elderly woman sat down, obviously frustrated, angrier than before, and looking about ready to explode with disbelief.

Why had her anger grown? Was she still mad about the lost test results? She probably was, but most likely that was not the reason for her continued frustration.

It didn't help that she had to take time out of her day to come back in, but I doubt that was the cause of her anger, either.

I truly believe the frustration, anger, and, yes, escalating rage she was now fighting to control was the very same thing that made me wonder why people skills are not consistently taught to customer, guest-, and patient-contact personnel.

Allow me to explain. In fact, please pardon me for a moment while I imitate the late comedian Sam Kinison in order to make the point. Here it is . . . SHE WANTED TO BE ACKNOWLEDGED! She was saying, "ACKNOWLEDGE ME! . . . UNDERSTAND MY FEEL-INGS! . . . THAT'S ALL I WANT FROM YOU!"

She wanted the receptionist not just to know what had happened but also to understand her feelings. She wanted her to say, "Oh dear, I'm so sorry that happened. You must be terribly upset. Well, I'll tell you what—I will personally make sure everyone here on staff is aware of it and it won't happen again. I'm so sorry."

She wanted to be shown some empathy!

I can practically guarantee you that had the nurse said that (regardless of what had actually happened), the woman would've become a big fan and huge promoter of the company.

The receptionist's polite, by-the-numbers, and totally impersonal response ignored the woman's feelings, ignored her dignity.

Sure, it probably wasn't the receptionist's fault the records got lost but that's not the point.

Fault wasn't the issue. And expecting the customer or patient to understand the workings of the company's systems and procedures is totally counterproductive. The onus is on the business personnel to understand this and take the lead.

While no one should ever be expected to take abuse from those they are in business to serve, incidents such as these can be so easily handled that it seems like a waste of personnel (not to mention really effective marketing) not to do so correctly.

So let's ask ourselves, when someone voices a complaint regarding something we or anyone within our company has allegedly done . . . or not done, do we—regardless of the facts—at least let them know we understand they are upset? Do we communicate that a remedial action will be taken? And do we—to the degree we have the power to do so—display empathy in such a way that says, "You matter"?

Because they *do* matter! And they need to know.

CHAPTER

64

JUST LISTEN

Listening is so vitally important to the influence process. Influencers listen—sometimes, they *just* listen. Not problem solve. Just listen.

While certainly there are times when proactively helping someone solve a problem is very legitimate, paradoxically, not trying to solve a problem is often the best way to have it solved.

By simply listening and allowing the other person to be heard, the problem often simply dissolves. After all, sometimes people just need to be heard—to voice their feelings and talk them through. Or, just as well, the person solves the problem themselves, which empowers them and makes them feel good about themselves.

I've had to work very hard at improving myself in this area. It is unnatural to my being. When someone comes to me with a problem, I still have to fight my inclination to go into fix-it mode and, instead, I just listen.

On a speaking trip there was a logistical mix-up in one city that caused some slight inconvenience. Although it was truly not a big deal to me, it caused some negative feelings for the meeting planner, who felt that it looked as though she had dropped the ball. She wanted to speak with my business partner, Kathy, and me personally in order to bring some closure to the situation.

We did a three-way conference call and she began to relate the story from her point of view. Wanting to put her mind at ease, I began to share that I knew she was not to blame and that all was fine. I thought it would make her feel better.

Yet, sounding frustrated, and as though she couldn't help herself, she began to talk over me.

Suddenly, I noticed an IM pop up with a message from Kathy. It simply said: "Bob, I think she really just needs to be listened to right now."

Point taken. Kathy was right. The meeting planner simply needed to be heard. She had been frustrated by feeling that her actions had been misunderstood and simply needed us to listen. Satisfied that was now the case, all was fine.

Sometimes the most influential thing we can ever do is listen. Just listen.

CHAPTER

REMEMBER TO SCRATCH THE HOGS

n the classic *My Voice Will Go with You* by Sydney Rosen, there is a story in the foreword by Dr. Lynn Hoffman that reaches the very essence of persuasion.

> [There was a time] when Erickson, who as a young man sold books to pay his way through college, was trying to sell some to a crusty old farmer. The man isn't having any and tells Erickson to go about his business. Erickson, without thinking, picks up some shingles from the ground and starts scratching the backs of the hogs the farmer is feeding. The farmer changes his mind and agrees to buy Erickson's books because, as he says, "You know how to scratch hogs."

I see two valuable lessons in this. The first is that, sometimes, the best way to persuade, once a person says no, is by not *trying* to persuade. Just be nice. Be a "person."

This builds up feelings of like and trust. Instead of feeling pressured, they feel relaxed. They like you. And they now begin to trust you.

The second lesson also has to do with building trust. It is the principle of Similarity.

Simply put:

People tend to intuitively trust those who are like them.

Picture it: young Erickson comes by selling books. Perhaps he was wearing a suit and tie—"dressed to sell," but not to a farmer in his work clothes. No relate-ability. You can almost hear the farmer thinking *city slicker.* In actuality, Erickson grew up on a farm.

Now, however, after dismissing the young man, the farmer notices that Erickson, without thinking, simply begins to scratch the hogs in a way that only a farmer would know. By this one simple act Erickson created relate-ability and instant trust. All of a sudden, the books became something to consider. Talk about buying emotionally rather than logically!

Relate-ability is accomplished most easily by finding similarities.

Yes, opposites might, on some level, attract because differences can be interesting.

But to inspire like and, perhaps more important, trust, highlight your similarities with the other person.

So when someone says no to you, don't fight with them. Instead, pick up a shingle and "scratch some hogs."

CHAPTER

66

THE PRE-APOLOGY APPROACH

As I approached the ticket counter, the agent did not look happy. In fact, he looked downright miserable. This was not a good sign. I needed to change a couple of items on my ticket, and time was of the essence. But this was a man who, by the looks of things, was prepared to be difficult. I knew I had to be very effective in very little time to end up with a winning situation.

First, I approached him with a genuinely warm, friendly smile. While this alone is usually helpful, in this case it had no visible effect whatsoever. I have to admit, I really felt like telling him to shape up and get with it! Of course, doing that would have just turned a potential adversary into an *actual* adversary.

Instead, I decided to gently disarm him by using what I call the pre-apology approach.

"I'm sorry you've got to even bother with all this stuff, it must be a real pain in the neck."

It was that simple. From there he went above and beyond for me. All he needed was for someone to empathize, to communicate an understanding of what he was feeling. With that one small statement his attitude completely shifted. I'll bet he was friendlier to the customers that followed me, as well.

The natural *reaction* would've been to match his scowl, but the inevitable battle would have only led to lose/lose. It's always easier to get what you want or need by first helping the other person feel good about themselves, and about you.

The key to the pre-apology approach isn't the apology but the empathy. Look and listen for what they're feeling, even if they're unaware they're communicating it, and acknowledge it.

The next time you encounter a potentially difficult person, remember that the pre-apology approach will help to quickly turn things in your direction.

A Tiny Bit of Empathy Can Go a Long Way

Emails such as the following, whether after a blog post or a live speaking event, totally make my day. Notice how this reader took the information you've been reading and simply applied it to his own unique situation.

> Bob—I had a situation a few weeks back at a hotel in New Orleans. We had paid far in advance for a room with a king bed, but when we arrived it was two doubles. When we went back down to the front desk, we were informed that there were no kings available. I could sense that I was at the emotional crossroads! Lol. I noticed myself getting angry and ready for a major confrontation, BUT, I took a breath, relaxed and regrouped, and remembered your advice about creating the expectation of cooperation.
>
> So I shifted my approach, released all the tension, and shared some understanding for the challenge of the gentleman at the front desk (this was just a week after hurricane Isaac, so things were a bit out of sorts).

The upshot? We not only got the room, but we made a great friend in this front desk gentleman, and he helped us in so many other amazing ways to have a spectacular stay!

Next time we visit (which will be soon!), we will have this awesome friend to insure everything is awesome . . . and we'll get to reconnect with him again. Small shifts in mind-set and approach yield giant results!

And honestly, this is about much more than simply gaining a satisfactory outcome, it's far more about finding ways to interact with other human beings in a positive and mutually beneficial/enjoyable fashion.

And for that piece of awesome insight, I extend a giant thank you to you Bob!

And I thank *you* for sharing that with us!

67

INFLUENCING IN STYLE:
A READER SUCCESS STORY

This letter, from Margaret in Missouri, is an excellent example of a person who has truly learned and internalized the principles we've been discussing throughout the book.

Hi Bob, I wanted to thank you and to tell you about something that happened just recently.

I'm traveling soon (work related) and wanted to stay at a bed and breakfast. I contacted the inn by email with specifics about when I would need lodging and the price I was looking to pay ($90.00). The owner responded that there was a room for the specified dates but that the rooms were $95.00. Not wishing to hurt the owner's feelings, but really wanting them to lower their prices so it would be possible to stay at the Inn, I sent the following email message:

Thank you for getting back to me. Your inn seems lovely from what I have read and seen on the Internet. I imagine anyone staying with you would be thoroughly satisfied with the quality of accommodations provided.

Unfortunately, I will not be able to stay at the inn because the rate of $95.00 exceeds the company's lodging allowance of $90.00. I feel your inn is well worth the $95.00 per night, but I cannot change the company's limit that I may spend.

Should you have a rate change in the next two weeks, please contact me.

Again, I thank you for your timely response to my inquiry.

Well, the owner sent me an email the next day saying:

We can do $90 for you. Please call direct so we can book your room. Thanks.

Isn't that wonderful?! I feel like it was a win for both of us.

Wow, didn't Margaret handle that tremendously? Don't let the fact that it involved only five dollars per day fool you. What she did works in all situations and with much higher financial stakes. Let's review.

1. **Positive frame.** As she said, she didn't wish to hurt the owner's feelings. She wanted the owner to feel good about the transaction. That attitude alone is an excellent way to *frame* the process, as it communicates the desire for a win/win exchange.

2. **Begin with gratitude.** In her follow-up email, she didn't argue but began by thanking the owner. And it helped to diffuse any possible defensiveness the owner might have had in learning that a potential guest wanted the fee reduced.

3. **Compliment.** She complimented the inn profusely. This inn is undoubtedly a great source of positive identification and pleasure to the owner. Margaret's compliment most likely meant a lot! And who wouldn't want someone with such good taste and appreciation to stay as their paid guest?

4. **"I couldn't justify."** When she lets him know that she can't take the room, she reassures the owner that this decision has nothing to do with him or the inn. The price is over her budget and she has no choice. (We saw in chapter 53 the "I couldn't justify" method.)

5. **The out.** And this was beautiful. She kindly and gently requested that *if* there happened to be a rate change, to please let her know. She didn't try to paint him into a corner with an ultimatum. That way, agreeing to her terms was his idea, not something he felt manipulated into doing.

Awesome!

SECTION SEVEN

The Character of Ultimate Influencers

Even More Important Than What You Say and What You Do Is Who You Are

Character may almost be called the most effective means of persuasion.

—Aristotle

John Allison, the former chairman and CEO of Branch Banking & Trust Company (BB&T), grew one of the most profitable banks in the country. It was also one of the few banks that did not involve itself in subprime lending, writing only conventional loans.

Mr. Allison understood the unholy alliance between many politicians, government-sponsored entities (such as Fannie Mae and Freddie Mac) and many of the banks. And being that this was contrary to the principles upon which he and his bank stood (making a profit through providing value to their clients), the decision to forgo the countless easy billions being made by his peers was clear.

When everything came crashing down, his bank was left standing tall, both in profitability and reputation.

The kicker is that eventually he was *forced* by the government (under thinly veiled threat) to take bailout money he neither needed nor wanted.

He is no longer in the banking profession. Mr. Allison is now a distinguished professor at Wake Forest University School of Business and CEO of the Cato Institute, a libertarian think tank.

John Allison stood for something. After all, that's what people of character do.

People with a high amount of influence practically always have a high level of character. As mentioned early in the book, people will allow themselves to be influenced by those people they know, like, and trust. And it's much easier to trust someone when you know where they stand and what they stand for.

In this section, we'll look at character and its very strong relationship with Ultimate Influence.

STAND FIRM ON PRINCIPLE

Groucho Marx, one of our greatest comedians, said, "Those are my principles. And, if you don't like them . . . I have others."

What a comical reflection on a sad reality. A person's character is their defining quality. Perhaps, more accurately, it's the sum total of all their qualities. I believe that when you really understand a person's character, you can predict their major decisions.

They are consistent. They are predictable. In this case, a *good* predictable.

While the media gives significantly greater attention to those whose principles are along the line of Groucho's above persona, fortunately there are many more whose principles—based on high character—are indeed immutable.

And those are the Ultimate Influencers.

THE MASTER OF "GOODSPEAK" . . . AND INFLUENCE

My Dad, Mike Burg, introduced earlier, is the greatest Ultimate Influencer I know. From as early as I can remember, he was making people feel genuinely good about themselves, helping them become more self-confident, and simply better human beings. He did it as part of his business, and he did it in his personal life. And though long retired, he's still the same person doing things the same way.

While I've read books on the topic and studied people skills, persuasion, and influence for a long time, it's true that (to paraphrase the title of a famous book) all I really needed to know about influence and persuasion I learned from my Dad.

The following is something I wrote many years ago. I now post it on my blog every year on Father's Day as a way to say thank you. The story has made its way around the Internet and has even been included in a couple of other books.

As human beings, we have the ability, and the choice, to lift people up or to put them down. And we don't even have to speak to them directly in order to do either. The person I try most to emulate is my Dad. He's always had the most amazing gift for making people feel good about themselves. Yes, I *try* and emulate Dad and that amazing trait, though I've never been able to do it to the degree he has (though, he'd tell me different).

Dad's ability isn't only finding the good in everyone, but also verbalizing it. He's mastered building people both directly and to others. While many people gossip, Dad finds and speaks the good. When he must correct, it's always with tact and kindness.

Many people relate to others the bad spoken of them, creating conflict. Dad always relates the good someone said about them, bringing people closer together.

Have you ever heard husbands, when speaking to others, make unkind remarks about their wives? It's one of those *macho* things, right? Sure, they're "only kidding," but words matter. Examples, good and bad, are set, especially for children.

Growing up, I always remember how Dad spoke so glowingly of Mom, as did she of him (they *still* do!).

My Parents began poor and built a successful business. Although Dad was the one in the public eye and Mom more comfortable behind the scenes, Dad always made sure everyone knew who he considered to be the true driving force behind the business.

My favorite "Dad story" took place when I was 12. We were having carpet installed in our home. The crew boss was one of those stereotypical beer-guzzlin', hard-livin' guys, who would have probably belonged to Ralph Kramden's Raccoon

Lodge from the old *Honeymooners* TV show (nothing wrong with that—just painting a picture).

For lunch, my folks bought pizza for the crew. Dad went to talk with the boss about the job. I was around the corner listening.

The boss said, "This is an expensive job. Women will really spend your money, won't they?"

Dad responded, "Well, I'll tell you, when they were right there with you before you had any money, it's a pleasure to do anything for them you possibly can."

This wasn't the answer he expected. The boss was looking for negative talk about wives, which, to him, was normal. And, Dad, with his open, relatable personality and the natural "street way" that never fully left him, probably seemed like someone with whom the crew boss could bond.

He tried again, "But, gee, they'll really play off that and spend all they can, won't they?"

Dad replied, as I knew he would, "Hey, when they're the reason you're successful, you want them to do the things they enjoy. There's no greater pleasure." Strike two.

The crew boss tried one more time, sort of stumbling, "And . . . uhhh, they'll take that as far as they can, huh?" Dad responded, "She's the best thing that ever happened to me. I'd do anything to make her happy."

I was trying not to laugh. I knew he wanted Dad to give in just a little bit and say, "Yeah, I guess that's true." But I knew that wouldn't happen—not in a million years!

Please understand; my Dad was never condescending. He was simply himself; a person who loved and respected his wife so much that there is no way he would give in and participate in that type of talk.

Finally, the boss gave up. Maybe he learned something about respecting one's spouse. Maybe not. But it taught a young boy a lot about the power of respect and edification.

Mom and Dad, at the time I'm writing this, have been married 56 years.* They still hold hands, and are more in love than ever. In fact, they adore one another. They are truly best friends. Would there be any doubt?

While this story focuses on a loving couple, it's not just about that. There's a reason my Dad has had such influence on the lives of so many people.

What you read about Dad is simply who he is. And because it's who he is, it's what he does.

---

* Of course, that's brought up to date every year I post the story.

FOCUS ON YOUR STRENGTHS
BUT DON'T IGNORE YOUR WEAKNESSES

How can you influence others if you are not aware of exactly what you *bring to the table*?

Some personal development advice tells us we should ignore our weaknesses and focus only on our strengths.

While there's certainly much validity in focusing on our strengths, to ignore our weaknesses can be downright dangerous to our potential success and influence.

Our strengths are the values, talents, and positive characteristics we bring to the marketplace, as well as to our personal relationships. They are the foundation of our influence. Focus on them, indeed. However, ignoring your weaknesses can be potentially destructive.

Is procrastination a weakness of yours? If so, it's most likely holding you back big time. What about impatience with others? If yes, then it is stifling the influence you might otherwise have with those you wish to lead. Anger? If that is a weakness of yours, you must already know how destructive that is in terms of your level of success. Those are just three biggies.

I believe that our personal weaknesses can be grouped into three main categories.

1. **Those that truly do not matter.** For example, I'm not good at running long distances. Since I have no plans to run a marathon, I ignore that one.
2. **Those that matter and need to be mitigated.** I have a weakness for junk food and have to be very aware, constantly monitoring myself. Of course, I could take that a step further and eat extra healthy. But I don't. Instead, I just eat healthy.
3. **Those that matter and need to be turned into a strength.** I was a gossiper. That one I worked on until I not only overcame it but became well known for very rarely saying anything negative about anyone.

Had I not overcome that last one and turned a weakness into a strength, I can guarantee you that my level of influence and success in *many* areas of my life would be less than it is now. Another weak point for me was my anger issues. That's another one I had to work hard to overcome. Once I did, it made a huge difference in my life and my ability to build trust and influence with others.

Benjamin Franklin understood this concept and devised his own Character Improvement program, which he shared in his autobiography. The difference that it made in his life is self-evident.

So, yes, by all means, focus on your strengths. That's where you will achieve the most.

But don't ignore your weaknesses. At least the ones that matter.

IGNORE PROBLEMS AT YOUR PERIL

One reason the five principles discussed in this book are so important is because the real difference between most people and Ultimate Influencers is their ability to solve problems. The world rewards greatly those who can solve problems. In order to do that, you must face them head-on. The principles in the book show you how, but your willingness to acknowledge those problems comes first.

As we said in the previous chapter, focusing on the positive does not mean ignoring the negative.

Life brings us problems; business brings us problems. While these problems should not be our focus, we do need to recognize, acknowledge, and deal with them.

At the same time, once you come up with a plan for finding a solution to your problem, focus on that plan.

In other words . . .

Acknowledge the problem, but live in the solution.

Again, we often hear or read that we should simply ignore the negative, that which we don't want. Well, I believe that while it's terrific to think positively and *focus* on the positive, *ignoring* the negative is not a good direction to take. The reason is that . . .

What is ignored does *not* necessarily go away.

Don't get me wrong; as usual, there is a time and place for most everything. And there is indeed a time to ignore what simply doesn't serve you.

But sticking your head in the sand like an ostrich to hide from your problems is not productive. And that's the best case. At worst, it will cause the issue to fester and grow bigger.

So note that there is a problem. Acknowledge that the problem is there. Devise a game plan for overcoming it—determine the solution. And then focus on that solution.

But don't ignore the problem. If it needs to be dealt with, that's up to you, the Ultimate Influencer.

WHY TOP INFLUENCERS BUILD STRONG TEAMS

My great friend the leadership authority Dan Rockwell says:

If you know more than everyone on your team, you have a weak team.

True leaders and influencers not only *accept* having smarter and more knowledgeable people on their team, they *seek them out*. They purposely surround themselves with people who are more capable than they are in one or more specific areas.

On the other hand, *positional* leaders (those simply in a position of authority), tend to derive their self-esteem from their status. As a result, they'll defend any perceived threat to their role either consciously or unconsciously. However, this defensiveness also can, and usually does, sabotage their influence.

True leaders praise and credit these talented team members for all the value they provide them and the organization. They also actively look for ways to allow these people to lead and to shine.

While leaders can come from anywhere within an organization, I've always found that the culture of an organization begins at the top and trickles down. When the executive team is guarded and defensive, that's typically the tone throughout the organization. The opposite is also true.

Only a leader with character, competence, and *confidence* desires to be surrounded by those he or she deems to be in some way superior. And that leader tends to have very strong teams as a result.

CONSISTENCY—A PRIME INGREDIENT OF TRUST

We live in an inconsistent world, filled will many well-meaning but inconsistent people. Thus, in business—in life—consistency removes uncertainty and leads to trust. Trust, in turn, leads to influence.

The person who manages to show up authentically day after day, week after week, month after month, and even year after year builds a bank account of trust that will pay dividends for as long as they keep making those deposits.

The man or woman who delivers on their promises consistently, when they say they will, and without excuses keeps their clients and enjoys an army of *personal walking ambassadors* like few others.

And the level of influence they have with others is correspondingly high.

Anything and Everything

There's a related aspect of consistency that is just as important, and that is consistency of effort.

There's a saying that, for many years, has been one of my personal favorites.

In *Secrets of the Millionaire Mind*, T. Harv Eker says:

How you do anything is how you do everything.

This is one of the most important principles for an Ultimate Influencer to follow.

One of my greatest heroes, Booker T. Washington, credits one of his first employers (and a true mentor), Mrs. Ruffner, with changing the course of his life. She taught him why when he swept her floor clean, it needed to be done 100 percent, spotless, with nothing missed. This turned him from a young up-and-comer with great *potential* into a man who would accomplish more and change more lives than most people could ever even imagine.

In his famous Tuskegee lectures, Dr. Washington taught this valuable success principle to his students and protégés. Imagine if this one thing—doing your best every time and in everything you do—were taught everywhere.

CHAPTER

74

GROWING FROM YOUR MISTAKES

E ven top influencers make mistakes. They don't like to. I don't
know many people who do. Mistakes can be downright uncomfortable.

However, when you can admit you made the mistake, take full
responsibility for it, and then correct it to the best of your ability, you
have taken a giant step in your personal growth as well as in your
ability to influence others.

It starts with admitting it. Many people cannot or *will not* do that.
Ultimate Influencers do that!

> Being able to admit you are wrong is not only one of the first
> signs of maturity but perhaps the foundation of any type of
> growth and effectiveness.

It is also the sign of one with high character.

Yes, mistakes are a key to growth, if you are first able to admit
them, and accept responsibility for them.

75

SELF-CORRECTION—WHEN YOUR REPLAY SHOWS YOU FUMBLED

Successful people are not only open to hearing about their mistakes via both solicited and unsolicited feedback but find ways to provide themselves with needed feedback, as well.

Does this conflict with the fact that those of high character tend to stand very firm on their guiding principles? Not one bit. There is also no natural dichotomy on being principle based and admitting one is wrong. Nor in staying principle based while adjusting your strategy.

As Zig Ziglar so wonderfully said, "Be firm on principle but flexible on method."

Hopefully, you have people around you—friends, colleagues, family members—who are willing to give you feedback when you've messed up. If you're an Ultimate Influencer, those close to you should feel comfortable approaching you about these sorts of things. I know I rely on others to point out my mistakes and fumbles. It makes me a better person.

Still, we can't always rely on others to do this for us. Ultimate Influencers know that while we should always listen to thoughtful criticism, it's often hard to come by. So what do we do? We correct ourselves.

"But, Bob," you ask, "aren't we simply too close to the situation to see things objectively?"

Indeed, it can be difficult to be objective with ourselves. But focusing on self-correction helps you understand yourself better and be more prepared to notice when you've messed up. When you do that, you can take steps to rectify the situation, or at least make sure it doesn't happen again.

For example, if you say something hurtful to a cashier at the grocery store, you will probably recognize her look of anger or sadness. Recognizing that something is clearly wrong, and that this person is definitely still an adversary, you can pause to reflect on something you may have said or done to make her feel bad. If so, you can apologize. It may not always be easy—especially if you are angry or stressed—but the more you do this, the better you'll get.

Form the habit of asking yourself, *How did I handle that difficult interpersonal situation*? Or the objections during your one-on-one sales presentation. Or the challenging questions from the committee member during your group presentation. Were you able to make the person feel comfortable by being tactful, empathetic, and kind, while still effectively and persuasively communicating your point? Or did you kind of *fumble* that one? (As we all do, from time to time.)

Study it; dissect it. The trick is to do so with as much honesty and as little emotion as possible, focusing on not letting your ego take over. Yes, it can be difficult. Make that . . . very difficult. And it's well worth it.

Make the decision to learn from your mistakes and—hopefully—not repeat them. At least not too often. If you're like I am, you most likely will repeat them until you have the lesson learned. Then again, that's part of what being human is all about.

And one more thing. Aside from realizing the mess-ups, recognize your victories, as well. You will have plenty of those. Take pleasure in them. Celebrate them.

76

WANT TO BE AN ULTIMATE INFLUENCER? SAY LITTLE AND DO MUCH

The Sages of the Talmud wrote, "Say little, do much, and greet everyone with a pleasant countenance." And when it comes to becoming an Ultimate Influencer, this is especially true.

People with Ultimate Influence are people of character. And people of character do what they say they will do. Establish a reputation for saying little, always coming through on your promises, and then over-delivering on them. Do this consistently and success in business and in life is yours.

Develop a reputation as a person who, rather than *talking* a good game, actually *plays* a good game. One who, instead of *talking* about being honest, *is* honest. Instead of *talking* about thinking of others, *thinks* of others.

Say little and do much, and others will feel confident in following your influence.

And, of course, don't just read the information in this book and then put it aside. Apply the information and become the person of Ultimate Influence you were meant to be.

ACKNOWLEDGMENTS

I remember many years ago listening to a very famous speaker at a conference who, partway through his presentation, looked out at the audience and authoritatively declared, "If it is to be, it is up to me!"

We applauded enthusiastically at his lesson on personal responsibility.

In the very next session, an equally famous speaker, partway through *his* presentation, and with an air of benevolence, said, "Nobody does it alone!"

We applauded enthusiastically at *his* lesson on the importance of teamwork.

In the hallways and assorted gathering places afterwards, there was much discussion about those two "opposing" thoughts. However, they are not opposing at all, are they? Rather, they represent one of those magnificent paradoxes of life: when two seemingly divergent statements or philosophies fit together beautifully. In other words, it's not an either/or, but an *and*. Nowhere is this more true than in the process of writing a book. At least for me it is.

Yes, if it's going to happen, I need to take responsibility for my part of the process.

However, there's absolutely no way I could ever do something like this alone. It's the help, teamwork, advice, encouragement, and counsel of those I'm honored to have as part of my life as well as those whose wisdom I can refer to via their writings that makes any of my books possible. Perhaps more so in this book than in any other I've written.

So, while I'm going to mention a number of names, please know that this is a very incomplete list of thanks. I really could fill an entire book; it's only my faulty memory and space limitations that keeps it as brief as it is. If you're someone who should be mentioned here and is not, I ask for your forgiveness. To quote George Costanza, it's not you, it's me.

Margret McBride, the best literary agent in the business (prejudiced though I may be) and her phenomenal associate, Faye Atchison: I appreciate you both being a part of my life for these last seven years. You always have my back.

Adrienne Schultz: Thank you for the painstaking amount of time you put into helping me clean up the first draft. I was amazed when—immediately afterwards—it actually reminded me of a book.

The team at Portfolio (current and past), to whom I still refer as "Team Go-Giver": Katie Coe, Allison McLean, Jacqueline Burke, Brittany Wienke, Brooke Carey, Courtney Young, Maureen Cole, Will Weisser and of course, El Jefe, the phenomenal Adrian Zackheim—I can't imagine a publisher being more supportive of an author. I love all of you. And a special shout out to Natalie Horbachevsky, who did a fantastic job of holding my hand and walking me through the final process. And, thank you to Patricia Nicolescu, who did a terrific job with the copyediting. Great saves!

Dr. Thomas Gordon, whose work introduced me to the I-message, which has been an important part of my life as well as my teaching; and the large number of today's teachers, researchers, and practitioners on conflict resolution, whose books I've enjoyed and from which I've learned so much.

Dr. Adam Grant, a new but *very* valued friend. Thank you for your help and advice, as well as your fantastic book, *Give and Take*. Through your exhaustive research and reader-friendly style, you answered so many questions regarding an individual's motivation and actions. You are the epitome of what John David Mann and I would call a "Go-Giver."

A few of my political mentors also rate as some of the most powerful, positive and classiest persuaders I've ever had the privilege to know and learn from: Dr. Mary Ruwart, Michael Cloud, Sharon Harris, and the late Harry Browne. Harry, you are so missed.

Dr. Robert Cialdini, your book, *Influence: Science and Practice* is nothing less than genius. It explained the hows and whys of influence in a way that brings a very deep level of understanding to all of us who have studied it.

Several people, some with us and others no longer, mentioned in the book whose teaching has really helped me, either with specific concepts or general, overall wisdom. They include Don Miguel Ruiz, Dr. Maxwell Maltz, Dr. Gary Chapman, Daniel Goleman, Dr. John C. Maxwell, Dr. Paul Swets, Pastor Dan Rockwell, Rabbi Moshe Goldberger, Vernon Howard, James Redfield, Les Giblin, Donald T. Phillips, and Dr. Stephen R. Covey.

Stephen M.R. Covey, thank you for your passionate and insightful work on Trust. It's difficult to imagine a topic of greater importance and your books, *The Speed of Trust* and *Smart Trust* have both qualified and quantified its tremendous importance.

Dondi Scumaci and Susan Solovic: thank you for being so extraordinarily cool, kind and gracious.

John David Mann: my coauthor in *The Go-Giver* series, a great guy whose talent and brilliance is overshadowed only by even more of his talent and brilliance.

My MasterMind group, including Randy Gage, Lisa Jiminez, Patrick Stinus, Terry Brock, Gina Carr, Joachim de Posada, and Bruce Turkel: those all day-long and into-the-night sessions have been a wealth of knowledge and wisdom, as well as some of the biggest laughs one can imagine. How great it is to be able to talk freely and disagree about all those things that we are absolutely, positively never supposed to discuss in polite company.

Carrie Zaatar, Michelle Colon-Johnson, Ilene Courtenay: you are the most amazing team members that a guy with a speaking and writing habit could ever hope to be associated with.

The team of Certified Go-Giver Coaches: you are all a joy and I'm so very grateful for having you in my life. You are spreading the message, my friends, and I appreciate you more than you can imagine.

To my speaking clients: Thank you. Without you, I would not have an audience, nor the pleasure of being involved in such a rewarding career.

The late, Zig Ziglar, one of the world's great human beings. Your work was the first to show me just how related selling is to . . . *everything* in terms of working effectively and benevolently with others. I love seeing what your proud son, Tom and the next generation of Ziglars are doing in keeping your legacy alive and flourishing.

Kathy Zader, my best friend and business partner: you totally and continually astound me both by everything you are and by everything you do. I so lucked out when I met you!

A special tip of the hat to the late, Dale Carnegie: you got this whole genre started. *How to Win Friends and Influence People* has created a much better world for all of us.

And, of course, my thanks to you, the reader, for your participation, feedback and encouragement. I wish you the best of success and may you turn any and all potential adversaries into your strongest allies.

INDEX

UNLEASH THE POWER OF INFLUENCE IN YOUR TEAM!

Bring Bob in to speak at your next company or organization's conference.

–MOST REQUESTED PROGRAMS–

- ➡ Adversaries into Allies
- ➡ The Go-Giver/Go-Givers Sell More
- ➡ Endless Referrals

Bob combines humor and entertainment with hard-hitting, immediately applicable information that will inspire your team and give them both the tools and confidence to succeed.

Bob's many clients include General Electric, UBS, New York Life Insurance Co., Aflac, RE/MAX, and Million Dollar Round Table.

Here's what just a few of Bob's clients have said afterwards:

"A lot of thought goes into who we invite to speak at our international conferences. In a competitive sales environment, Bob's was a great choice, right on the mark and exactly what our team needed. His vast experience, knowledge and a very engaging style brings outstanding value with the information he provides. No matter how high-tech the world has become, business success is still all about the relationships. Bob is the best in teaching exactly how to build them."
> **—Subroto Bagchi,** Chairman, Mindtree Limited, Bangalore, India

"Many thanks for the outstanding job you did for our client, RE/MAX. My client was so thrilled after the first 15 minutes that she actually left the room to call me. Your ideas were spot on. You obviously did your research. You took that stage and delivered 100%."
> **—Derek Sweeney,** President, The Sweeney Agency

"As the keynote speaker at our national meeting, Bob's message was powerful and so very much needed in today's business environment. While we asked him to speak because of what he had written (we love *The Go-Giver* and *Go-Givers Sell More*) his ability to deliver the value came from his genuine desire to listen to us, to hear us, and to gear his presentation to exactly what we needed. Both Bob's message and his actions made a lasting impact on our organization."
> **—Monte Salsman,** COO, WinWholesale, Inc.

To schedule Bob call 866-962-6995 or 775-220-6995
www.burg.com